D0878694

GOD IS NO DELUSION

For my mother and my father

Thomas Crean O.P.

GOD IS NO DELUSION
A Refutation of Richard Dawkins

*A magnitudine enim speciei et creaturae
cognoscibiliter poterit horum creator videri.*

For by the greatness of beauty and of
the creation, the Creator of them may be seen,
so as to be known thereby.

Wisdom 13:5

IGNATIUS PRESS   SAN FRANCISCO

© 2007 Family Publications, Oxford
All rights reserved
Reprinted in the U.S.A. by permission of Family Publications

Cover design by John Herreid

Published in 2007 by Ignatius Press, San Francisco
ISBN 978-1-58617-231-2
Library of Congress Control Number 2007933599
Printed in the United States of America ∞

Contents

Preface

This book is a reply to Professor Richard Dawkins' recent attack on religion. Professor Dawkins is an opponent of all religions. This book, however, is not a defence of all religions: it would not be possible to write such a defence, since the various religions of the world are incompatible with each other. It is a defence of two things. First, it is a defence of theism: not merely an argument that one may reasonably believe in God, but an account of why our author's philosophy, atheism, is false. Secondly, it is a defence of the particular religion to which I adhere, namely, Catholicism (the same religion, incidentally, that founded and named Professor Dawkins' own college[1]). It is not, however, a systematic apologia for Catholicism, simply a reply to the various charges that the author alleges against us.

The first two chapters of this book are more philosophical and therefore slightly more abstruse than the succeeding ones. This is unavoidable, given their subject: the possible cause or causes of our visible universe. Still, though they may require closer attention than the other chapters, I hope that they will be accessible to the general reader. On the other hand, I have not attempted to anticipate all the philosophical questions that might be raised about my arguments, for example, how the universal

---

[1] 'The New College of St Mary', Oxford.

causality of God is compatible with free will or with sin. To have done so would have taken this work too far from its goal: the rebuttal of Professor Dawkins' attacks.

St Thomas Aquinas once observed that when opponents of our faith do not recognize the authority of any part of our holy scriptures, our unique recourse must be to 'natural reason, to which all are bound to assent'. It is in this spirit that I offer the following pages.

Thomas Crean O.P.
Passiontide 2007

Chapter 1

PROFESSOR DAWKINS'
ARGUMENT

Professor Richard Dawkins, the eminent biologist, has written a book purporting to show that belief in God is a delusion.[2] I do not think it would be unfair to say that his book contains only one argument for this conclusion. Of course, it contains many other statements about religion, as also about morals, biology, physics, anthropology and children's education. But it seems to offer only one argument for atheism. This is the argument I shall examine in my opening chapter.

Preliminaries

What does Professor Dawkins mean by 'God'? He summarizes what he chooses to call the 'God Hypothesis' as follows: 'There exists a super-human, supernatural intelligence who deliberately designed and created the universe and everything in it, including us' (p. 31). A Catholic has no fundamental quarrel with this way of stating the question. True, for reasons of reverence we should not normally speak of God as simply 'an intelligence', but rather as the supreme intelligence, or as intelligence itself. But this is a relatively minor point.

---

[2] R. Dawkins, *The God Delusion*, London, Bantam Press, 2006.

Again, though acknowledging that God is 'super-human', in the sense of 'more perfect than mankind', we do not normally use this word of him, since it is insufficiently precise. Angels, too, are super-human, yet they are not God (Professor Dawkins, of course, may not believe in angels: but this is beside the point). Similarly, the exact sense of the word 'supernatural' in this definition is unclear. If it simply means 'what is superior to the reality perceptible to bodily senses', it again applies to God, but not to him alone. Angels, as pure minds, are imperceptible in principle both to our sense-organs and to those of all other bodily creatures. For these reasons, we might prefer to replace the Professor's summary of theism with the following: 'The whole universe, including ourselves, was designed and created by the supreme and uncreated intelligence,' whom we call God. However, for present purposes, nothing significant turns on these different ways of stating the question.

An 'argument from complexity'

I have claimed that Professor Dawkins offers only one philosophical argument for atheism. It could be called 'the argument from complexity'. His idea is this: if a being existed with the attributes generally said to belong to God, such a being would be complex, and therefore would require a cause. He writes:

> A designer God cannot be used to explain organized complexity because any God capable of designing anything would have to be complex enough to demand the same kind of explanation in his own right. (p. 109)

Professor Dawkins is saying to us, in effect, 'Do you think

that because the universe is so complicated, God must have designed it? But just think how complex God must be if He could have designed the whole universe! Who designed Him, then? Better to say the universe had no designer after all.'

How should we answer this? Before offering a more serious reply, we could point out that even were this argument sound, it wouldn't invalidate the author's own summary of 'the God Hypothesis'. This 'hypothesis' was that our universe has been designed by an intelligence distinct from itself. The argument from complexity would not prove that there was no such intelligence. Were it sound, it would simply show that any such intelligence must have a cause which was not itself intelligent. And that intelligence may arise from non-intelligent causes, is, of course, one of the main tenets of our author's *Credo*.

However, this is something of a debating point. For our author might naturally reply that theists consider it essential to the notion of God that He is the *First Being*. Therefore he could state his case more carefully in these terms: 'God is supposed to be both the intelligent designer of the universe and also the first being; but any intelligent designer of the universe would be so complex as to require a cause outside itself; therefore there can be no God who is both an intelligent designer and also the first being.'

Assessing the argument

The Catholic philosopher will wholeheartedly agree that complexity always demands an explanation. Whenever different things are joined together, whether the atoms in a water molecule or the various thoughts in the mind of a philosopher, some explanation of the 'joining together' is always needed. Complexity is not self-explanatory. Professor

Dawkins was once invited in a newspaper interview to complete the sentence 'In the beginning was. . .'; he replied with the word 'simplicity'.[3] St Thomas Aquinas would have approved of this answer.

But why does our author claim that no designer of the universe could be simple? No proof of this proposition is attempted. It is put forward rather in the manner of a self-evident truth. Reading between the lines, however, one can discern in the author's mind two relevant considerations, one drawn from the natural world, the other from the world of information technology. The following is a fairly typical remark:

> God may not have a brain made of neurones, or a CPU made of silicon, but if he has the powers attributed to him he must have something far more elaborately and non-randomly constructed than the largest brain or computer we know. (p. 154)

One could draw out the argument as follows. In the natural world, the more complex a product is, the more complex will its producer be. Men build cathedrals, which are very complex; birds, endowed with smaller brains than men, build nests, which are considerably simpler than cathedrals; single-celled organisms build neither cathedrals nor nests. Therefore, the universe, being the most complex of all visible things, must have been built, if at all, by a being much more complex than a man.

Or again (the argument would run), maybe the hypothetical designer of the universe is more like a computer than like a living thing. But the more powerful and efficient a computer is, the more complex must be

---

[3] *The Independent*, December 4th, 2006.

its circuitry. Any computer powerful enough to design and make the universe would need to be exceptionally powerful; *ergo*, it would have to be very complex.

So in either case, whether the designer of the universe were more like an organic being or more like a computer, he would have to be very complex and so he could not be the First Being. This is the argument of Professor Dawkins' book.

The argument is insufficient

The argument just described, by which our author thinks to prove the non-existence of God,[4] is an example of *induction*. By induction, one examines some individual things of a particular category in order to reach a general law applicable to all things of that category. For example, having ascertained that various portions of water boil at 100 degrees Celsius, one can formulate the general law, 'water boils at 100 degrees'.

However, in order that an argument by induction may be sound, its conclusion must not extend more widely than the evidence warrants. For example, I can't argue, 'This European has two legs, this Asian has two legs, this African has two legs, therefore all mammals have two legs.' The correct conclusion would be that all men, by nature, have two legs. Since all my examples of bipedalism were taken from the human species, I can't use them to formulate a general law for all mammals.

Why is this relevant to Professor Dawkins' argument? All the examples of complexity that he mentions come

---

[4] He himself speaks (p. 109) of proving not the impossibility of God's existence but only its extreme improbability. However, if the designer of this universe were a complex being, he could not possibly be the First Thing.

from the realm of *bodily things*. Animals and computers both fall into this category. Therefore a correct conclusion might have been: 'So long as we remain within the realm of bodily things, complexity of producer increases with complexity of product.' But according to the theist, of course, God is not a bodily thing. He is Spirit. The Professor's induction is therefore entirely irrelevant. The complexity of the universe has no tendency to show that a designer of the universe who was not a bodily thing would be complex.

Can a designer be simple?

Our author might reply that, all the same, there is nothing in our experience to show that it is likely, or even possible, that even a non-bodily designer could be simple rather than complex. But is this true? We can approach the question in a circuitous way, thinking first not of designers, but of *designs*.

Is a design, as such, something complex or something simple? Imagine an architect overseeing the building of a cathedral. The architect has a design of the cathedral in his mind. He has an idea of it which he sees slowly realized before his eyes. Which is simpler, the idea of the cathedral or the cathedral itself? Consider the following points.

We can talk about the north or east side of the cathedral. Can we talk about the north or east side of the architect's idea? No: an idea has no sides, nor does it face a particular direction. In this respect, at least, the idea or design of the cathedral is certainly simpler than the cathedral itself. It doesn't have different sides facing different points of the compass.

Again, the cathedral is composed of different materials. One part will be made of stone, another of glass or lead and so on. Is the idea of the cathedral made of all these various materials? Obviously not: an idea isn't made of anything at all. One can have the idea of a stone, but not a stony idea. Even the most thorough-going materialist, who says that ideas are somehow *generated* by the movement of tiny particles in our brains, would scruple at saying that an idea is made of electrical impulses as a cathedral is made of stones.

So, while the cathedral is made of many different kinds of stuff, the idea isn't made out of any kind of stuff at all. Here is another sense in which, in comparison with the cathedral, the idea or design of it in the architect's mind is remarkably simple.

The cathedral is also complex in other senses. It has a shape, perhaps that of a cross. The idea of the cathedral, on the other hand, has no shape. We can have an idea of a cross, but not a cross-shaped idea. Again, the various parts of the cathedral will stand to each other in different proportions: for example the floor of the baptistery may occupy an area one quarter that of the sanctuary. The idea doesn't have any such complexity. It makes no sense to say that one part of my idea of a cathedral has the same surface area or volume as another part. An idea doesn't have parts in spatial relation to each other: only the thing of which it is an idea has parts.

An idea, whatever it is, is clearly something very simple. It has no size, shape or mass. It has no constituent parts standing in spatial relation to its other parts. It can serve as a design for something complex, but in its own nature it is free of the complexities that it represents. How this is so is rather mysterious to us. But no one can deny that it is so.

The idea or design of a material thing, then, is much

simpler than the thing of which it is a design. What does this show us? It shows that there is no reason to suppose that a designer must always be as complicated as the thing that he designs. A designer, strictly speaking, is just 'a being with a design'. So since a design is something very simple, as the example of the cathedral shows, a designer is just a being with something very simple. So there is no reason why he himself should be complicated.

Professor Dawkins would have been correct if he had stated, not that the designer of a complex product must himself be complex, but rather that a designer must be at least as *perfect*, at least as 'rich in his reality' as the thing that he designs. The designer must be at least as 'rich in reality' as the thing he designs, because before he produces it, he must first possess it within himself in a certain way. He must 'have' it in an intellectual way, in order to cause it to exist in the material world. In this sense, a designer must have the same 'richness' as what he makes. But he need not have the same *complexity*. The idea of a cathedral is as rich as the cathedral, in the sense that it contains, in an intellectual way, all that the cathedral is. But it is much simpler than the cathedral.

Someone might retort that the architect himself is more complex than the cathedral, even if his idea is not. Yet this isn't because the architect is a designer; it's because he is a *human* designer. As a human being, he needs a complicated body for receiving and processing sense data before he can formulate ideas within his mind. But an intellectual being, such as an angel, that had ideas without deriving them from sense data, need not have a complex body. Such a being could therefore possess a design of some complicated thing, such as a cathedral, whilst being much simpler than the thing he designed. To be a designer, that is, to have a design or an idea present to one's mind, is as such something very simple. In man it requires highly complex preconditions. But there is nothing at all in the *notion* of design, or a designer, which implies complexity.

Must an omnipotent God be complex?

Professor Dawkins has another, slightly different, formulation of the 'argument from complexity' to offer us. This relies not on the notion of design, but on that of activity. He expresses the argument, if such we may call it, as follows:

> A God who is capable of sending intelligible signals to millions of people simultaneously, cannot be, whatever else he might be, simple. Such bandwidth! (p. 154)

A believer may be tempted to respond that the author is conceiving of God as some kind of a machine, and hence that his remark is a mere grotesque irrelevance. However, the argument might be expressed more philosophically as follows: 'Anything which can perform several actions at once must be complex. But God, as conceived of by theists, can perform several actions at once. Therefore he must be complex.'

This argument, like the preceding one, might be sound if we supposed that God were a bodily thing. A bodily thing, at least in our ordinary experience, acts on other things by material contact: all or part of the first bodily thing is brought, directly or indirectly, into material contact with all or part of another bodily thing in order to act upon it. Therefore in order to act on more than one thing at the same time, it must have different parts. A human being can pick an apple from a tree whilst kicking a ball because he has both hands and feet. But since God is not a bodily thing, the argument fails. In whatever way spirit acts on matter, it is not by material contact, since spirit is defined as 'what is free of matter'. So there is no reason to suppose that because God can cause several things to happen simultaneously, He must therefore be complex.

According to the theist, God acts on creation not by means of bodily organs or electronic apparatus, but simply by his will. Now an act of will is simple in just the same way as an idea. If I will to do something, for example to build a cathedral, it makes no sense for someone to ask 'What shape is this volition of yours, of what materials is it made, what colour is it and how heavy, in what direction is it facing, and what are the relative proportions of its various parts?'

Of course we human beings aren't generally able to get things done by acts of will alone. But this is because the other things in the universe don't depend on us for their existence. So it's not surprising that we should be unable to change them just by willing to, and without making use of our bodily organs. But if there is a Will on whom the universe depends for its very existence, it would not be surprising if a single act of that will could by itself cause the universe to change.

After all, even we can cause some things to exist simply by willing them, for example, thoughts. If I choose to think of justice, or the square root of two, then without further ado these thoughts exist. My mind is, in this sense, dependent on my will. So if the universe is dependent on God, as the theist claims, why should not God be able to cause things to exist within it simply by willing them to exist? And however many things He willed to exist, His act of will could still be simple, just as with us an act of will is simple even when it bears on something complex, like a cathedral.

An objection

At this point, Professor Dawkins might object that I am making things too easy for myself. True, he might say, an idea or an act of volition, seem very simple considered in themselves. But don't we know that they depend necessarily on the presence of a highly complicated brain? I spoke above of an angel who would have ideas without needing to form them from sense-data 'processed' by a nervous system. But isn't that a purely gratuitous hypothesis? Don't we know that ideas, thoughts, volitions and other so-called 'mental events' are inescapably bound up with matter?

In other words, doesn't modern science force us to take a *materialist* view of reality? To this question I now turn.

Materialism defined

By materialism, I mean the following philosophical position: 'Everything that exists is either matter or else a property of matter.' The materialist doesn't refuse to talk about minds or thoughts or choices. But he holds that none of these things would be possible without matter. He maintains that every mind or thought or choice either is matter or else is a property of matter.

Note first that this is indeed a *philosophical* position. It is not, in the modern sense of the term, a scientific one. No amount of research into the material world can give grounds for the denial of an immaterial world, just as no amount of research into the Alps can be a rational basis for denying the existence of the Sahara. Prolonged researches into the topology of the Alps might make the Sahara desert seem very vague and distant to the researcher, but that is simply a fact about the human mind, which has no implications for geography. In the same way, prolonged researches into the world of organic life might make the researcher feel that the world of spirits was something implausible or absurd; but his feeling would be without rational value.

Two questions arise. First, is materialism necessary? Next, is materialism possible?

Is materialism necessary?

That materialism is necessary is a very strong claim. It is equivalent to saying: 'Nothing could possibly exist except what is made of matter or else is a property of matter.' Does Professor Dawkins hold this position? It is hard to say. He certainly approaches it, by quoting with apparent approval the following passage, taken from the eighteenth century American politician, Thomas Jefferson:

> To talk of immaterial substances is to talk of *nothings*. To say that the human soul, angels, gods, are immaterial, is to say that they are nothings, or that there is no god, no angels, no soul. I cannot reason otherwise ... without plunging myself into the fathomless abyss of dreams and phantasms. (p. 42)

The French philosopher Jacques Maritain once wrote that to disbelieve in angels was a sign of feeble-mindedness. Jefferson's words are a good illustration of this maxim. The 'founding father' of the United States offers no shadow of a reason why an immaterial substance could not exist. He merely dogmatises that what is immaterial is nothing, and that nothing independent of matter can have any real being.

A Catholic philosopher would say that Jefferson was a prisoner of his senses. He didn't manage to rise above what he could see, hear, taste, smell and touch. All our knowledge certainly begins with what we learn through our five senses, but it is not limited to this. So a person with sufficient strength of mind will see that the notion of being and the notion of what is perceptible to the senses are two different notions, and that there is no necessity for the first always to be joined to the second. 'Being' simply means 'that which is'. It doesn't imply any necessary relation to the senses, any more than the term 'animal' implies any necessary connexion with the term 'winged'. Some animals are winged, others are not. Some beings are perceptible to the senses, either directly or else by means of instruments, but there is no reason why all should be. There is nothing in the notion of being that requires it.

For more than nine-tenths of his book, Professor Dawkins gives the impression of being a thoroughgoing materialist. Early on, he quotes approvingly some words of a like-minded author, that 'atheists believe that there is only one kind of stuff in the universe and it is physical' (p. 13).[5] Later he states categorically:

---

[5] In fact, a Catholic philosopher is also likely to believe that there is only one kind of stuff in the universe. Spirit is not a kind of stuff: it is not 'an indeterminate something' that can be a constituent of many different substances, as matter can. To use the word 'stuff' in this context, where what is evidently meant is 'real being', indicates that not only does one not accept the existence of spirit, one has not yet grasped the very notion.

> A dualist acknowledges a fundamental distinction between mind and matter. A monist by contrast, believes that mind is a manifestation of matter – material in a brain or perhaps a computer – and cannot exist apart from matter. (pp. 179-80)

He then declares himself 'a dyed-in-the-wool monist'.

A surprise is in store, however, in the last chapter, where the author turns his attention away from religion towards physics. Here the reader is warned:

> We have this tendency to think that only solid, material 'things' are 'really' things at all.... We find 'real' matter conformable to our understanding only because our ancestors evolved to survive in the Middle World,[6] where matter is a useful construct. (p. 370)

If matter is only a useful construct, what remains of the claim that everything in existence is made of 'physical stuff'? Even more puzzlingly, he quotes with approval another author's claim that since the atoms that make up our bodies are in a constant state of flux, therefore 'whatever you are, you are not the stuff of which you are made' (p. 371). Plato could not have put it better.

Is Professor Dawkins recanting his materialism in this final chapter? It seems impossible that a dyed-in-the-wool monist should endorse the remark, 'Whatever you are, you are not the stuff of which you are made.' However, I don't wish to read too much into a single sentence, especially when this forms part of an extended quotation from another author. By this point, as well, Professor Dawkins has given the reader fair warning that he has passed from logic to rhetoric (p. 361). It is wise as well as charitable to

---

[6] By this phrase is meant the world discernible to our senses, as distinct from the realms of the very large and the very small.

assume that an author is consistent with himself, unless the contrary evidence is overwhelming. Still, if our author is indeed an orthodox materialist, he provides no argument for his position. No argument is offered in defence of the proposition that all things must be things accessible to the senses. He does not even try to show us that materialism is necessary.

Thinking about thoughts

If materialism is not necessary, is it even possible? We can approach this question by reflecting on the human mind, and in particular on thoughts.

According to the materialist, what is a thought? If all that exists is either material or else a property of matter, there are only two possibilities. A thought must either be something material, such as electrical impulses moving between cells in the brain; or it must be a property of something material, as colour and shape are properties of a rose. Which option does our author prefer? Neither is explicitly chosen. Instead, we read that 'human thoughts . . . *emerge* from exceedingly complex interconnections of physical entities within the brain'(p. 14, his italics). But we should not let the spurious profundity of the word 'emerge' bamboozle us. A thought is something real. A man who is thinking about genes, for example, is different from a man who is not thinking about genes. So what is this real thing, this thought? If we are materialists, it must be either a material thing or a property of a material thing. So which is it to be?

Let us begin by assuming that a thought is a material thing. It is an electrical impulse in a brain cell, or rather, some very complex arrangement of electrical impulses in a large number of interrelated brain cells. Now is this identification, between a thought and electrical impulses in a large number of brain cells, coherent: that is, does it make sense? It's certainly possible, sometimes, that two things which we identify independently of each other should later turn out, much to our surprise, to be identical. For example, we can read in the newspapers of some wanted criminal, learning about his methods and habits, and one day discover to our amazement that he is our next-door neighbour. These 'two' men, our neighbour and the criminal, seemed to us to be entirely different individuals, and yet later they're revealed as identical.

Or again, imagine that someone sees at twilight what appears to be a small tree on the other side of field. He knows a certain amount about the object, for example, its approximate size and shape. Going closer, however, he finds that it is not a tree at all but a good friend of his. 'Two' things that seemed to be entirely different, the dark shape glimpsed across the field and the friend, are revealed to be just one thing. Is it possible likewise that a thought about the weather, say, and a group of electrically stimulated brain cells, two things that seem quite different, should nevertheless turn out to be the same?

A crucial difference exists between this last suggestion and the two other surprising identifications that I imagined. If my next-door neighbour turns out to be a master criminal, I may be very surprised, but I understand perfectly what is meant by the identification. After all, I always knew that the criminal had to be some human being or other, and my next-door neighbour is a human being, so from the logical point of view it is quite coherent that my neighbour should be the criminal, however respectable he may have seemed. Likewise, all the man knows for certain about the black shape across the field is that it is a medium-sized object, rather taller than it is wide; and if his friend is also a medium-sized object of this kind, then although the man may be momentarily startled when he sees that the shape is his friend, the identification will cause him no kind of logical or metaphysical bewilderment.

Things are very different with the putative identification of my thought about the weather and an arrangement of electrical impulses in my brain. It is not that I should be surprised if I found that they were identical; rather, I can assign no sense to the suggestion. In what sense could a number of electrical impulses *be* my thought that it will be a sunny day tomorrow? My thought is about the weather. How can an electrical impulse in a brain cell be *about* anything? It is itself, not something else.

Thoughts are not material things

In order to 'turn out to be identical', two separately identified things must at least share some common category. My next-door neighbour and the criminal mentioned by the newspapers were both men, so their identification was possible. The black object in the field and my friend were both medium-sized material objects, and so their identification was possible. What common category can be found for a 'complex inter-relation of physical entities in my brain' and a thought? Perhaps someone will say that they are both 'realities'. But this is not a category, since it doesn't serve to distinguish one kind of thing from another. It gives us no means of understanding the proposition that 'my thought *is* this inter-connexion of electrically-charged brain cells'.

After all, if two things are the same, then their properties must be the same. The top half of the black object across the field will be the top half of my friend, if my friend is the black object. So if the electrical impulses in the brain cells were my thought, then three-quarters of them would be identical to three-quarters of my thought. But what is three-quarters of a thought? What would count, for example, as three-quarters of the thought 'it will be a sunny day tomorrow'?

Or again, if electrical impulses passing through brain cells were my thought, the spatial relations of the different impulses would be identical to the spatial relations of the different parts of my thought. But what spatially related parts exist in the thought 'it will be a sunny day tomorrow', or the thought 'nothing in excess'? Or again, the various electrical impulses in my brain are moving from one place to another. But when I think, for example, 'it will rain tomorrow', does this thought also have many parts moving from one place to another?

In a word, to identify thought with electrical impulses in the brain or with brain cells or with any other material thing leads to absurdity.

Thought is not caused by matter

The absurdity of identifying thoughts with any material thing explains why the materialist philosophers followed by Professor Dawkins prefer to say, not 'thought is matter', but rather, 'thought emerges from matter'. But what is the meaning of the word 'emerges' here? Perhaps it means 'matter is one kind of thing, and it causes thought to exist, which is an immaterial kind of thing'. Note that if this is the meaning, then the materialist case has been silently abandoned. If thought is an immaterial kind of thing, then it is obviously false that everything which exists is material.

More importantly, how could a 'material kind of thing' cause an 'immaterial kind of thing' to exist? How would it go about it? Material things have parts that can be re-arranged to form new things, but the new things are always just as material as the old ones. For example, sulphuric acid and copper are both material things. If the acid is poured onto the copper, something new will come into being, copper sulphate. Some of the ions have been taken from the acid and joined to the metal to make this new thing, which, naturally, is just as material as they are. And however complex the material things are that one starts with, and however much they are re-arranged, they can never yield anything other than a material thing. So if thought is an immaterial thing, no interaction of material things will ever bring it into being. Clearly, when Professor Dawkins tells us that 'thought emerges from matter' he cannot mean that a material thing causes a non-material thing to exist.

Thought is not a property of matter

What else can be the meaning of the phrase? Its only other possible meaning is that 'thought is a property of matter'. According to this theory, once a sufficiently large number of brain cells has been gathered together and stimulated in some way, thought 'supervenes' on these cells as a property of the whole group. But 'supervening' is here a word without an idea behind it. For how can a material thing possess a property unless the property affects it in some material way? A material thing can possess the properties of blueness or hotness or squareness, since it can be made blue or hot or square. But how can a material thing possess the thought 'tomorrow will be a fine day'? It is not changed by this thought in any material way as it would be changed by blueness or squareness. A thought 'makes no difference' in the material world. It does not change the shape or colour or size of anything. How then can a thought be possessed by a material thing as one of its attributes? There is no conceivable relation between them. It is as if one were to say that the number two could be heated by a Bunsen burner.

Materialism, then, is absurd. A thought cannot be a material thing, nor can it be caused by a material thing, nor can it be the property of a material thing. The only possible conclusion is that thought as such is something independent of matter, that is, something *spiritual*.

I say thought as such, since it is obvious that for human beings, thought presupposes certain material conditions. We did not need the discoveries of modern neuroscience to know that someone who receives a sharp blow to the head may for a time be unable to think. The Catholic philosopher will say that this is because man is a unity of body and soul. In this life, the soul is not sufficiently free of the body to function unless the body itself is co-operating by providing the sense data which are the raw material on which the mind works. But since thinking is neither identical to, nor a property of, nor caused by any material thing, this dependence of thought on the right disposition of the brain is a merely *extrinsic* dependence. It is not intrinsic to the nature of thinking as such. To take a distant analogy: some buildings may need to be buttressed from without in order to remain standing, but there is nothing in the notion of 'a building' to require that every building be buttressed. Most stand on their own foundations. In the same way, human beings during this life need a brain of a certain kind in order to think, but there is nothing in the notion of 'thought' to require that all thought must be 'buttressed' by a brain.

It is therefore quite possible that beings should exist which think, but which have no dependence on any material thing. Such beings, we have seen, would be far simpler than human beings; that is to say, not less rich or perfect, but rather, less complex, made of far fewer parts. For thought as such, whether it is the thought of a thing one intends to make, or a thought about something that already exists, is extremely simple.

Simplicity need not mean imperfection

At the heart of our author's philosophizing is a confusion of two different notions: simplicity and imperfection. The simpler something is, he believes, the more imperfect must it be; the fewer its parts, the fewer its functions. But this is only true for as long as we remain within the visible world. In this visible world, the better things are, the more complex they must be. A dog, for example, which is more complex than a single-celled organism, is also superior to it. It can do more than the cell, and do things that are more interesting. Unlike the dog, the cell cannot bury a bone or go to fetch a newspaper. The cell in turn is more complex than a single molecule and can perform activities, such as growth and reproduction, of an altogether higher order than the molecule. It is obvious, in fact, that in the material world, greater power is conferred by a greater variety of components, provided these are integrated into one whole. So those, like Professor Dawkins, whose principal study is material, living things, will be especially prone to think that complexity and perfection are correlative or even identical terms.

But when we pass from the material world into the world of knowledge, there is no longer a correlation between complexity and perfection. In fact, the reverse is true: there is a correlation between simplicity and perfection. We have already seen that our knowledge of a material thing, such as a cathedral, is much simpler than the thing itself. It is also *better* than the thing: for who would deny that the act of *knowing something*, which is what a thought is, is better than being a mass of stones, however beautiful? Likewise, the better our knowledge, the simpler it will be. For example, intellectual knowledge, by which we form concepts enabling us to reason and to communicate, is better than the sense-knowledge that we share with the other animals. If we were limited to the individual data that we receive from the five senses, having no power to form general concepts based on what we learn by the senses, we should have no speech, no natural science, no philosophy. All these things are made possible by intellectual knowledge, not by sense knowledge alone. Yet intellectual knowledge is much simpler than sense knowledge: to see a million oak trees would require a vast number of different sense-impressions; the thought 'a million oak trees' can be conceived all at once; it requires no multiplying of experiences.

Even within the kinds of knowledge proper to human beings, increased powers go hand in hand with greater simplicity. A musical genius such as Mozart can grasp the whole movement of a symphony at a stroke, in a single moment of artistic inspiration. The student who studies this same symphony will have to go through it laboriously, bar after bar, multiplying his thoughts in order to grasp Mozart's musical idea, and even so his knowledge of it will no doubt be far inferior to its composer's. Or again, any teacher knows that a brighter pupil will grasp some principle quickly, whilst a less bright child will need the teacher to multiply examples in order to see the teacher's meaning. For example, the brighter child will understand straightaway the principle, 'Do unto others as you would have them do unto you,' whereas the slower pupil will need the teacher to give several examples, perhaps about cheating or lying or stealing, before the principle sinks into his mind. It is a sign of greater intelligence to understand something by means of fewer examples, that is, in a simpler manner.

In other words, in the realm of thought, greater simplicity is a mark of greater perfection. The better the knower, the simpler his manner of knowing. Far from supposing, then, that a being perfect enough to know and design the entire universe must be extremely complex, we ought to suppose that he would be extremely simple. Nor should it bother us if we cannot imagine what his knowledge would be 'like'. A dog, whose knowledge is limited to what his senses can perceive, could not imagine how any being could have 'a million oak trees' as a *single* object of knowledge. For him, an oak tree is something that he looks at or sniffs. Since he cannot sniff a million trees simultaneously, he cannot imagine how this number of trees could be known by a single act. We, who possess conceptual knowledge as well as sense knowledge, do understand how this is possible. But if we desired by means of our own experience to grasp the nature of the divine knowledge, we should be in the position of a dog trying by its own experience of the world to understand its master's thoughts.

A Catholic philosopher will say that God knows all things in a single act by knowing Himself. All things bear some resemblance to God: they are limited 'reflections' of His unlimited nature. Therefore, by knowing Himself He also knows all creatures that could ever exist. His act of knowledge is thus entirely simple. He does not have one thought about the stars, another about plants, another about mankind. God *is* one, eternal 'thought', by which He knows both Himself and all possible and actual creatures.

A question for materialists

I have just spoken of a 'Catholic philosopher'. But of course it is not only the Catholic Church with whom Professor Dawkins is in contradiction. He is fundamentally opposed to the tradition of wisdom that we owe to the ancient Greeks. He does not advert to this fact: the names of Socrates, Plato and Aristotle are not found in his extensive index (pp. 400-6). But it is as well to point out that his quarrel is not only with 'religion', but also with the greatest minds of antiquity.

What is the question at issue between our author on the one hand and the Catholic Church and Greek wisdom on the other? It is this: which is the ultimate reality, mind or matter? Professor Dawkins believes that it is matter; we assert that it is mind. Mind must have priority over matter, since it is simpler than matter, as the thought of a cathedral is simpler than the cathedral itself.

However, to those who hold that matter has priority over mind, and hence that mind is merely a product of matter, we can offer this further challenge. Consider any necessary truth: something that is not dependent on chance or on human choice, but which has to be the case. For example, we might take the proposition that the circumference of a circle is equal to twice its radius multiplied by π. Would this truth remain true if all material things were destroyed, or would it cease to be a truth?

If it would not be true in the absence of material things that the circumference of a circle equals $2\pi r$, then material things themselves must cause this to be true. But this is impossible. Material things are *subject* to this law; they don't create it. The circular cross-section of a tree trunk, for example, doesn't cause it to be the case that the circumference of any circle will equal $2\pi r$. Rather, even before the tree has grown, this law determines that the cross-section of its trunk will have this property. In other words, necessary truths are independent of the material objects that they govern. If there had never been a material universe, it would still have been true that the circumference of any possible circle will equal twice its own radius multiplied by π.

But if there had been no material universe, *where* would this truth have been? Would the number two, and π, and the radii and circumferences of all possible circles have existed by themselves in some spiritual realm? Such a suggestion makes no sense. If there were no material universe, these things could only exist in a *mind*. So if we agree that certain things are true independently of material things, we must admit that at least one mind exists independently of material things.

Perhaps the materialist will reply that when this truth about circles is said to be independent of material things, this doesn't mean that it would go on existing somewhere even if there were no material universe, but simply that if there is a universe, this truth will be verified of any circle within it. But he surely cannot escape so easily. Even if he doesn't allow that the proposition 'the circumference of a circle equals $2\pi r$' would remain as a truth in the absence of any material things, he has nevertheless allowed that the conditional proposition 'if there is a universe then the circumference of any circle within it will equal $2\pi r$' is true. The truth of this proposition must be independent of the actual existence of any universe, since it abstracts from questions of real existence. But how, according to the materialist, would it be true if no universe existed? In what would its 'being true' consist? Professor Dawkins imagines that if there were no matter, there would be nothing at all. But if there were nothing at all, how could there still be truth?

Failure of our author's intention

Our author intended to show that God's existence was 'very very [*sic*] improbable' (p. 109). Though he does not seem aware of the fact, his argument presupposes materialism. To undermine his argument, therefore, it would have been enough to point out that neither he nor anyone else has ever given any proof of this philosophical position. In fact, we have done more than this minimum, offering reasons why materialism must be false. Next, we shall consider some positive reasons for accepting God's existence, and see what our author has to say of them. This will occupy the next two chapters.

Chapter 2

PROFESSOR DAWKINS AND
ST THOMAS AQUINAS

Two paths to God

We can distinguish two paths by which one comes to know that God exists, one ordinary, the other extraordinary. The ordinary path starts from the natural course of events and rises to the knowledge of an unchanging, intelligent cause of the world around us. This path can be pursued philosophically, using learned language, as it was, for example, by Aristotle and St Thomas Aquinas. Far more often, however, people pass along this path quite spontaneously. They simply say, in these or similar words, 'there must be something behind it all'. It is not necessary to be a student of philosophy to reach God by this path. It is enough to have an intellect unhampered by sophistry or prejudice.

The extraordinary path starts with a miracle. An event occurs that could not have been performed by any of the natural agents at work in the world: for example, a man at the point of death is restored in a moment to perfect health. Such an event witnesses to the existence of a supreme being with power over this visible world. This path is called extraordinary in that only a minority of people witness miracles directly. Still, it can lead many people to God. On the testimony of a few trustworthy witnesses, many people may reasonably believe that a miracle has occurred.

Professor Dawkins wishes to close off both these paths to God; or rather, he claims that neither path is worth following. Let us see what his own claims are worth.

The 'five ways'

As many people know, St Thomas Aquinas stated that one could demonstrate the existence of God in five different ways, starting from five different features of the ordinary world around us. Professor Dawkins examines these ways rather briefly (pp. 77-9). The first three, he tells us, are just three different ways of saying the same thing. While this is not quite true, since they begin from different features of the world, they do have much in common. For the sake of brevity, then, I shall not examine all three separately, but only the first way, as representative of the others. Nor shall I consider the fourth way. This argument has baffled readers of St Thomas far more sympathetic than Professor Dawkins, and to attempt its elucidation would take us more deeply into metaphysics than is suitable here. Instead, we shall pass from the first to the fifth way, showing in each case how the existence of God can be known with certainty by reflecting on ordinary human experience. We shall also show that none of Professor Dawkins' objections to these arguments is valid.

How can there be change?

St Thomas' 'first way' begins with the fact of *change*. It is obvious, he writes, that many different kinds of change take place in the world. Things change their place, or their colour, or their size, or their relations with other things, and so on. Any kind of change would do as the starting-point of the first way, but I shall consider just one, namely *intellectual change*. A man begins to think of something, for example, Shakespeare. The moment before, he was not thinking about anything. Now a thought has come into his mind. In other words, the man has changed. This change, like any change, must have a cause, or otherwise it couldn't have occurred. So what caused this change?

Whatever it was that caused this change, it must either have changed itself in doing so, or not. Let's assume that the change in the man's mind is caused by something within him, for example, his will. He thought about Shakespeare because he willed to. But in that case, his will itself changed in order to cause the thought to arise in his mind. The man had not previously been choosing to think about Shakespeare. He had not been thinking about Shakespeare from the moment of his birth. But at a certain moment he does choose to do this: his will changes and causes the thought to come into existence in his mind.

Now, this change in the man's will, like the change in his thoughts, requires a cause. No event can occur without a cause, whether the cause can be known by us or not. And once again, the thing that causes the change in the man's will must either have changed in so doing, or not. If it did change when it caused the will to change, then it in turn requires some cause to explain the change that takes place within it.

But this process cannot go on indefinitely. If the man's intellect was changed by his will and his will by something else and that something else by something further and so on *ad infinitum*, there would be no sufficient explanation of the fact that the man has started to think about Shakespeare. There cannot be an indefinite line of intermediary causes with no first cause, just as a nail cannot be knocked into a wall by an unending series of hammers, each knocking against the next. There must be a first hammer wielded by some free agent. There must be a man at the beginning of the line who gives the impulse that is ultimately responsible for the movement of the nail.[7]

Likewise, there has to be a first cause of the man's thought. This first cause must be something that causes change without changing in itself. If it changed, it would need some cause outside itself, and so it would no longer be first. That's why the man himself can't be the first cause of his thought: neither his intellect, nor his will, nor his brain is unchanging. The same is true of all the material things that we see around us. All the things that we see, from acids to ant-eaters, change when they cause other things to change. The first cause cannot be like this: it must be beyond change.

What's more, the first cause of a thought must itself be something intellectual. Nothing can give what it doesn't have. A flame that boils water cannot be less than one hundred degrees hot. No teacher can instruct a class of children in maths unless he knows maths himself. A cause and its effect do not always appear very similar: if a man writes a book, the book needn't look like the man. But

---

[7] 'Ultimately responsible' within creation, of course. The man himself is not the first cause in absolute terms of the nail's movement. He changes in himself by wielding the hammer, and this change like any other derives from the wholly unchanging first cause, that is, from God.

there must always be as much reality in the cause as in the effect. No one can write a book, assuming it is his unaided work, unless the knowledge that appears in the pages of the book first existed in his mind. A cause must be at least as perfect as its effect, or else it wouldn't be able to cause it. That's why we can say that the first cause of the man's thought must be something intellectual: it must have at least the same 'intellectuality' as the thought itself.

In other words, the first cause must itself *be* a thought. But it must not be a thought that comes into existence at a certain moment. If it did, it would need a cause, and so would no longer be first. The first cause must be a thought that is always in existence, always 'actual'. Unlike our thoughts, it must not exist in a mind distinct from itself. If it did, something must have caused it to exist in that mind, and so, again, it would no longer be first. The first cause must be a subsistent thought. It must be a thought that exists of itself, eternally.

Such is St Thomas' 'first way'. Fifteen centuries before him, Aristotle had followed it to the same conclusion. It doesn't reach an absentee 'god', who is supposed to have given an initial fillip to the universe, and then left things to take their own course. It reaches the First Cause on whom everything now depends. Without such an unchanging First Cause, nothing could happen.

Professor Dawkins' objections

Although our author subjects St Thomas' first way to a critical scrutiny, I cannot be confident that he has understood it. His remark that a 'big bang singularity' (p. 8) would be more likely as a first cause for the universe than God suggests that he is thinking of a cause that is first in *time*. This is not the first cause of which Aristotle and St Thomas speak. While it is a point of Catholic faith that the universe had a beginning in time, this cannot be proved by philosophy. The first way would still be valid if the universe had always existed, as the following example shows.

Consider someone who is peeling potatoes. It's not self-contradictory to suppose that he has been peeling potatoes forever, and has by now amassed an infinitely large heap of them. From time to time, his potato peeler becomes rusty, and so he throws it aside and takes up a new one. It's not self-contradictory to suppose that he has by now amassed an infinitely large pile of rusty potato peelers. What would be impossible is that, to peel any given potato, an infinite multitude of implements should have to be used together, each one acting on the next. If, in order to peel any given potato, the potato peeler in contact with it had to be turned by another peeler, and this other by a third and so on without end, then one would never reach the man himself. If each instrument had to be put into action by another instrument, one would never reach the principal cause. But in that case, the potato would never be peeled.

In the same way, it's not obviously absurd to imagine, as Aristotle did, that the universe has existed forever in much the same way as it exists now. In that case, no cause would be first in time. Whatever man you chose, he would always have a father and a grandfather. Yet each individual change within that universe, for example, each new act of begetting, would still need a first cause. It would depend on something that didn't change when it caused other things to change. Without such an unchanging cause, it could not happen.

In other words, we do not deny the possibility of an infinite series of causes stretching back in time. What is impossible is an infinite series of causes at work here-and-now, in such a way that every cause, in its very action, would be dependent on another cause. Just as no potato could be peeled if every peeler had to turn another one, no change could take place unless something can cause changes without being changed. And this, St Thomas remarks, is what all men call God.

Yet this last point is precisely what Professor Dawkins is disposed to deny. Even though he seems willing to concede, rather grudgingly, that there may in some sense be a first cause of the universe, he remarks:

> There is absolutely no reason to endow that terminator [i.e. of the first way] with any of the properties normally ascribed to God: omnipotence, omniscience, goodness, creativity of design, to say nothing of such human attributes as listening to prayers, forgiving sins and reading innermost thoughts. (pp. 77-8)

This list of attributes is somewhat puzzling. Why is goodness not a human quality when the power to read other people's innermost thoughts apparently is? Surely this cannot be a reflection of Oxford academic life? More seriously, the first cause of a human thought, as we have just seen, must itself be something intellectual. It must be a subsistent thought, that is, an intellect 'in action' of itself. But such an intellect could have no limits, for, being the first cause, from where could it have received them? Nothing limited can be the first cause, because everything that has limits must have received them from somewhere. The first cause is an unlimited intellect. That is why omniscience is indeed a necessary attribute of the first cause.

In the same way, it is because God's nature is unlimited that philosophy must ascribe goodness to Him. Evil is not a positive reality, but a lack of some good quality that should be present, rather as blindness is not something positive, but the privation of the power of sight. Since God's being is unlimited, it can have no lack. There can therefore be no evil in God, but only in finite creatures.

We can also note that it is because God's nature is unlimited that there can be only one God. 'Another' god would have to lack something or other, for else he would not be distinct from the first God. But then, lacking something, his nature would be limited and he would not be God. Hence, there cannot be a great number of unchanging first causes, each responsible for different events in the universe. There can be only one First Cause because there can be only one being who is unlimited.

As for omnipotence, a being that is the first cause of any change that takes place in the universe, and which causes such a change effortlessly because without changing in itself, can hardly be denied this attribute.

The other attributes that Professor Dawkins mentions in his list are all consequences of the divine intelligence; though we can add that God's readiness to forgive sins is not something that can be deduced with certainty by philosophy alone. It is made known to us by revelation and remains in this life an object of faith.

Does St Thomas have an argument from design?

Now we come to the fifth way, which is often misunderstood. Indeed, our author takes to be his *bête noire*, the so-called 'argument from design'. As such, he announces, it has been invalidated by the theory of evolution (p. 79).

The argument from design, according to Professor Dawkins, consists in saying, 'Such-and-such a natural feature, say the eye, looks as if it has been designed. But things that look as if they have been designed must have been designed. Therefore the eye has a designer, who is God.' This argument, he believes, was routed by Darwin, whom he supposes to have shown that apparent design could result from a long, blind process.

Now, in this book I do not intend to consider the evolution hypothesis. I believe it is possible to present 'arguments from design' that are less facetious than our author's summary of them, and very convincing.[8] But such arguments would not be equivalent to St Thomas' fifth way. They can't lead us directly to God. They lead us to a designer, but they don't prove that this designer is God. The designer could be a created spirit, some being immeasurably more intelligent that any human person, but still finite. St Thomas' fifth way, on the other hand, does lead us to God.

Pace Professor Dawkins, this way doesn't start from the fact that some things look as if they had been designed, but rather from the fact that some things act even though they don't know what they're doing. For example, sodium, when placed into water, reacts with it in order to become sodium hydroxide. Obviously, the sodium does not say to itself, 'I ought to react with this water'; nor cannot it be said to act by instinct, as an animal seeks its proper food by instinct. It just acts, uniting the hydroxide ions in the water to itself.

[8] See, for example, *The Naked Emperor* by Anthony Latham, published by Janus. This book contains a chapter-by-chapter critique of Professor Dawkins' book, *The Blind Watchmaker*.

Why is this fact interesting to the philosopher? It is interesting because the reaction of the sodium with the water is clearly not a chance event. It happens whenever sodium and water are brought into contact. Sodium, we say, of its nature, has a tendency to act in this way. Even before a given piece of sodium is brought into contact with water, it has a predisposition towards performing this action rather than towards performing some other action, such as merely dissolving in the water. If it didn't, when it met the water it wouldn't react rather than dissolve. So the sodium has a certain relation towards this action; it is by its nature ordered towards producing this action rather than another, even before this action is performed. But how is this possible? How can the sodium have a relation towards an action that doesn't yet exist? A relation can only hold between two things that do exist.

The philosopher concludes that the action in question, before it comes to exist in the material world, must exist in some intelligence. It must exist in thought: it is only by thought that two terms can be related when one of them does not yet exist in reality. As St Thomas puts it: things that have no knowledge (like sodium) cannot be directed towards an end (such as reacting with water) except by something that does have knowledge. And things must have an end in order to act, for otherwise there would be no explanation of why they act in this way rather than in that, or indeed, why they act at all rather than remaining inert.

'But surely,' one may say, 'isn't it just the nature of sodium to react with water? Isn't this reaction sufficiently explained by the laws of chemistry? Why do we have to postulate some superior agent?' Yes: it is the nature of sodium to react with water. But what this means is, precisely, that before the sodium reacts, it already has a pre-determination towards this action rather than another. Yet it does not choose its action for itself, as an intelligent being may. Therefore, it must be directed to it by some intelligent agent. As for the 'laws of chemistry', this very expression indicates the presence of an intelligence behind the material world, for a law can only be instituted by a mind. When we speak of scientific laws, we are emphasizing that not everything in the world happens by chance, and that things have a predetermination to act in definite ways, like sodium reacting with water, even before they do act. Yet scientific laws by themselves, of course, cannot do anything. They cannot cause any event to occur. Only things can cause events to occur. And when the thing that acts is, like sodium, incapable of having intentions, some other thing must have assigned its action to it, to explain why it produces one action rather than another, or rather than none at all.

In other words, the fifth way relies on the 'Principle of Finality'. This principle states that every agent acts in view of an end. Unless an agent has an end, there is no reason for its action to occur, and so it will not occur. Just as an arrow cannot fly in a given direction unless it is first pointed in that direction, so sodium will not react with water to produce sodium hydroxide unless this end, rather than some other, has been assigned to it. If it had no end, it would not act.

This argument does have something in common with what is popularly called the 'argument from design'. Both start with some example of order in nature, and deduce the existence of a giver of order. But whereas men of the school of Professor Dawkins will explain the order apparent in, for example, the human eye, as the result of a long series of survival-enhancing flukes, no such escape is possible from St Thomas' fifth way. It doesn't depend on an order that might be claimed to have arisen from different beings struggling among themselves for survival. It depends on an order that is prior to any such interaction between beings; the ordering of any agent, animate or inanimate, to its own natural activity. Without this ordering, nothing could happen.

This 'fifth way' would be a sound argument even if there were nothing in creation but electrons moving in an atom. Since the electrons would not have chosen to move rather than not to move, nor how fast or in what direction to move, this must have been chosen for them. Unless some intelligence had assigned this motion to this electron, there would be no reason for the electron to follow this motion rather than any other. And if there were no reason for it to happen, it could not happen.

But why does the fifth way lead to God, and not, like an argument from design, simply to an intelligence? Imagine that the mind at work in nature was something finite: something like ourselves, having to understand reality by means of successive thoughts. In that case, when it came to think, it would be dependent, just like an inanimate object, on a superior intelligence. Just as a superior intelligence imposes a certain order upon nature so that natural things act in this way rather than in that, so a superior intelligence would have to impose an order upon this finite mind, so that it would think these thoughts rather than those. The superior intelligence would have to assign one kind of intellectual activity rather than another as the proper 'end' of the lower intelligence. Otherwise, the thoughts that arose within this lower intelligence would lack a sufficient explanation. Nor can we say that it would simply decide for itself what to think, because such a decision would itself be a thought, and hence require an explanation.

Therefore, any finite intelligence requires the existence of a superior intelligence to explain its own thoughts. But we cannot postulate an unending hierarchy of minds, each one having its intellectual activity assigned to it by the one above it. Just as there must be an unchanging cause of change, so there must be an 'orderer' that is not itself ordered by anything else. Some intelligence must exist that does not need to have an activity assigned to it. This is only possible if this intelligence *is* its own activity. The fifth way, then, brings us to a first intelligence that is one, unchanging, subsistent act of understanding. And this is God.

A last objection

Finally, and before turning to the question of miracles, we might examine Professor Dawkins' claim that the divine attributes cannot all exist together. He writes:

> It has not escaped the notice of logicians that omniscience and omnipotence are mutually incompatible. If God is omniscient, he must already know how he is going to intervene to change the course of history using his omnipotence. But that means that he can't change his mind about his intervention, which means that he is not omnipotent. (p. 78)

Clearly, it has escaped the notice of our author that real logicians refuted all such sophistries many centuries ago.

Omnipotence doesn't mean the power to perform any imaginary action that human beings might dream up, but the power to perform any action that does not involve a contradiction in terms. God cannot make a square circle, not because His power is limited, but because the notion of a square circle implies a contradiction. Again, God cannot sin, not because He is not strong enough, but because to sin is incompatible with the perfection of the divine nature. The notion of a 'sinful first being' is just as contradictory, though less obviously so, as the notion of a square circle. Likewise, God cannot change His mind, because the notion of a 'changeable first being' also implies a contradiction, as St Thomas Aquinas' first way makes clear.

According to Scripture, God has promised that certain things will never happen. For example, He has promised that a flood will never again wipe out all creation (Gen 8:21), and that the Church founded on St Peter and his profession of faith will not fail (Mt 16:18). But does this mean that He is no longer omnipotent, since neither of these events seems self-contradictory? Here it is customary to distinguish God's 'absolute power', or His power considered in the abstract, from His 'ordained power', or His power as 'ruled' by His wisdom.[9] God, absolutely speaking, has the power to send another flood across the face of the whole earth. The waters of the cosmos are still obedient to His will. But to send such a flood does not lie within His power as 'ruled' by His wisdom, because

---

[9] This distinction between God's power and His wisdom is a distinction only in our way of thinking about Him. In God Himself, there is no real distinction between power and wisdom, or between any of the divine attributes, since He is entirely simple.

He has decided that He will not do this. To take a distant analogy: a married man has the power, absolutely speaking, to leave his wife for another woman, but if he is wise, he will not leave her. Hence, if it could be guaranteed that he would always act wisely, we could say with certainty that this man, though he retains the radical power of leaving his wife, will not do so.

More generally, God has determined in His eternity above time how He will act at every moment of history. If we consider His power in the abstract, we can say that He is able to act otherwise than as He has decreed. But once given that He has actually determined to act in a certain way, He cannot then act in some other way. If He could, He would not be more powerful: He would no longer be God.[10]

---

[10] In the thirteenth century work, *On the Power of God*, St Thomas Aquinas answered Professor Dawkins' argument by anticipation as follows: 'The expression "God cannot do anything except what He knows that He will do" has two possible meanings. The limitation can be understood of God's power, or of His action. If it is referred to His power, the expression is false, since He has the power to do many other things than those He knows that He will do. If it is referred to His action, then it is true: but its meaning then is that it cannot be that something is to be done by God and that it is not foreknown by God that He will do it' (*De Potentia Dei*, Q.1, a.5 *ad* 1).

Chapter 3

PROFESSOR DAWKINS AND MIRACLES

If reflection on the world around us provides one great path to God, the other path is provided by miracles, whether witnessed by ourselves or reported to us by others. Our author explicitly recognizes the power of events reputed as miraculous to lead people to religious faith. He writes:

> Sophisticated theologians aside (and even they are happy to tell miracle stories to the unsophisticated in order to swell congregations), I suspect that alleged miracles provide the strongest reason many believers have for their faith. (p. 59)

I'm not sure of the identity of the sophisticated theologians to whom our author refers. The genial words that he puts into parentheses suggest that they would be men who themselves have no firm belief in miracles. Such men as St Augustine, John Henry Newman and Pope Benedict XVI would therefore presumably rank as unsophisticated theologians.

In any case, the Catholic Church certainly sets great store by miracles. Not only does she recognize that they take place today, she bases her entire preaching on a past miracle, namely Jesus Christ's resurrection from the dead. 'If Christ be not risen,' says St Paul in his unsophisticated way, 'then is our preaching vain, and your faith is also vain.'

A red herring

We can begin by disposing of a red herring. In the course of a passage where he is rightly rejecting the notion that Christianity involves no claims about the physical world – for as St Paul's words about the basis of faith show, it certainly involves the claim that the bones of Jesus Christ are not in the earth – Professor Dawkins says, 'miracles, by definition, violate the principles of science' (p. 59).

On the contrary, miracles do not violate the principles of science. If they did, it would be not only surprising, but inconceivable, that some believers in miracles should also have been great natural scientists. It would have been impossible, for example, that Louis Pasteur, the father of modern bacteriology, should have been also a devoted Catholic. It would have been impossible that Gregor Mendel, whom our author acknowledges as 'the founding genius of genetics' (p. 99), should have been a Catholic religious. (Professor Dawkins thinks to get over this difficulty by asserting that to join a monastery was for Mendel the obvious way to pursue a scientific career – in the nineteenth century!) It would be impossible that numerous other priests should have led the way in scientific research. We can find their names in the encyclopaedias: Fr Jean Baptiste Carnoy, the founder of modern cytology (the science of cells); Canon René Haüy, the 'father of crystallography'; Blessed Nicholas Steno, one of the founders of modern geology, Fr Lazzaro Spallanzani, the first man to explain digestion and animal reproduction, and who also helped to lay the foundations for vulcanology and disprove the notion of the spontaneous generation of cells. . . . Puzzling as he may find it, Professor Dawkins ought to admit that one can be both fully imbued with the 'principles of science' and a firm believer in miracles.

Really, one is almost ashamed to draw attention to such a confusion of ideas as our author's assertion involves. Natural science is a discipline that aims to discover the properties of bodily things and to express them as general laws. Miracles are actions of God by which He produces some effect without using any created cause. There is not the remotest contradiction between pursuing the former and believing in the latter. For example, it is a property of water that it has a surface tension, and that this surface tension can support some insects, but not the human body. A natural scientist can ascertain the surface tension of water by various experiments, and assign it a number on a scale. If he is a believer, he will accept that God, by His omnipotence, can preserve a human being upright on top of the water. He doesn't renounce his scientific knowledge by believing this. He doesn't begin to claim, in contradiction to what his own researches have shown him, that water has a surface tension sufficient to support the human body. He knows that it doesn't, as do we all. And so if he believes that St Peter, for example, once walked on the water, he will know that the water wasn't preserving him above the waves by its own nature, but God alone.

If we already accept the existence of God on other grounds, such as those mentioned in the last chapter, miracles will seem neither impossible nor unlikely. Not impossible, since God who is constantly acting in the world by means of secondary causes, as the unchanging cause of change, can certainly act without using these secondary causes. Creatures act directly on other creatures; I can pick a piece of paper off the floor; a bird can pluck a worm from the earth. By what conceivable principle would the Creator of the universe be unable to produce some effect without using any other cause, that is, to work a miracle? Not unlikely, since it is not unlikely that having made us, God would wish to communicate some message to us concerning the purpose of our existence. In what more suitable way could He authenticate such a message than by a miracle?

Investigating miracles

Professor Dawkins does not only object to miracles on 'scientific' principle. He also implies that there can never be a good reason in practice to suppose that a miracle has occurred. He quotes with approval (p. 91) a well-known assertion of David Hume:

> No testimony is sufficient to establish a miracle, unless the testimony be of such a kind, that its falsehood would be more miraculous than the fact which it endeavours to establish.

This assertion, as it stands, is quite true. But our author, like Hume, takes it to be equivalent to a second, very different statement: that miracles are so unlikely to occur that it is always more reasonable to suppose that those who report them are either in error or telling a lie, rather than telling the truth.

This second statement purely and simply begs the question. How, precisely, do we know in advance the unlikelihood of a miracle's occurring? What is the philosophical argument or scientific experiment that conclusively assigns to miracles this supreme degree of unlikelihood? Let our author answer if he can. If we already believe in God, we have a reason to expect that miracles will occasionally, though rarely, occur, for the reason mentioned in the last section. If we do not believe in God, but are not already convinced that God's existence is impossible or extremely unlikely, then we shall simply not know whether miracles can occur or not. We shall certainly have no *a priori* reason to deny them.

In fact, the testimony sufficient to establish a miracle is no different to that which establishes any event, namely a sane witness who is in a position to know the facts and who has no motive for lying. This is the testimony that the Catholic Church accepts in those procedures of beatification and canonization that so shock our author (pp. 59-60), though she takes the further precaution of putting the witnesses under oath. The rules of evidence do not change simply because an event is rare, or else how should we ever believe a report of a supernova, or a new comet?

A case study

Professor Dawkins makes a cursory examination (pp. 91-2) of the famous 'miracle of the sun' that took place in Fatima, Portugal in October 1917. I am not sure whether he is aware of the context in which this event took place. In May 1917, three Portuguese children, aged seven, eight and ten, claimed to have seen a Lady from heaven who spoke to them of sin and salvation and mankind's need to repent. They said that a miracle would take place on October 13th so that all would believe. They were laughed at or scolded by their families. When the story began to be talked about more widely, they were arrested and imprisoned by the local mayor, a Communist. He separated them and warned each one that he or she would be boiled alive in oil – and that the other two children had already been so boiled – unless the tale was retracted. Nevertheless, all of them persisted with the same story.

On October 13th, a crowd of 70,000 people gathered to see the miracle. It was by no means composed entirely of pious peasants: sceptical journalists were there in search of copy for a satirical article, as well as priests and academics, including one distinguished eye specialist. The children had told them to expect a miracle at around midday: of what sort, no one knew, not even the children. The vast crowd stood in the pouring rain for several hours. Shortly after midday, the clouds parted and they saw the sun turn different colours whilst apparently spinning on its axis. This lasted about ten minutes. Immediately after that, the entire crowd saw the sun plunge towards the earth. They were terrified. It seemed like the end of the world. Then they looked again, and the sun was in its accustomed place. Curiously, though they had been standing in the pouring rain for such a long time, each member of the crowd discovered that he was completely dry.

Hundreds of eyewitnesses testified to this event. Here are four testimonies.[11] First, from Dr Almeida Garrett, a professor at Coimbra University:

> The sun, a few moments before, had broken through the thick layer of clouds which hid it, and shone clearly and intensely. . . . It was a remarkable fact that one could fix one's eyes on this brazier of light and heat without any pain in the eyes or blinding of the retina. . . . The sun's disc did not remain immobile. This was not the sparkling of a heavenly body, for

---

[11] These testimonies are taken from 'The true story of Fatima' by John de Marchi, a full account of the relevant events. It can be read on-line at http://www.ewtn.com/library/MARY/tsfatima.htm.

it spun round on itself in a mad whirl. . . . The sun, whirling wildly, seemed to loose itself from the firmament and advance threateningly upon the earth as if to crush us with its huge and fiery weight.

Next, from Dr Domingos Coelho, the eye-specialist already mentioned:

The sun at one moment surrounded with scarlet flame, at another aureoled in yellow and deep purple, seemed to be in an exceedingly fast and whirling movement, at times appearing to be loosened from the sky and to be approaching the earth, strongly radiating heat.

Next, from Ti Marto, the father of the two youngest children:

We looked easily at the sun, which for some reason did not blind us. It seemed to flicker on and off, first one way, then another. It cast its rays in many directions and painted everything in different colours—the trees, the people, the air and the ground. But what was most extraordinary, I thought, was that the sun did not hurt our eyes. Everything was still and quiet, and everyone was looking up. Then at a certain moment, the sun appeared to stop spinning. It then began to move and to dance in the sky until it seemed to detach itself from its place and fall upon us. It was a terrible moment.

Finally, a journalist from *O Seculo*, then Portugal's most important newspaper and decidedly anti-Catholic, wrote simply, 'The sun trembled and made sudden incredible movements outside all cosmic laws.'

Here we have one of the most astonishing events in the history of the world. Three Portuguese peasant children predict several months in advance the precise day on which a great sign will take place. A huge crowd of people of all ages and conditions, comprising believers and non-believers, is gathered to the place where the children say that the miracle will take place. At the specified time, unprecedented, inexplicable and terrifying solar events occur. Tens of thousands of people witness this. Hundreds have left us their solemn testimonies, with not a single dissenting voice. Finally, by a last touch of divine providence, their sodden garments are dried in an instant by the heat of the sun as it approaches the earth, so that no one will be able to claim afterwards that he had suffered a visual hallucination. The reasonable conclusion is that a miracle did indeed occur.

Now, what does Professor Dawkins make of all this? He frankly admits that it may seem unlikely that so many thousands of people were simultaneously deluded or colluding in a lie, or that the detailed historical records that we possess concerning this event were somehow fabricated later on without anyone realising it. Does he therefore draw the rational conclusion? No: 'Any of these apparent improbabilities', he says, 'is far more probable than the alternative: that the Earth was suddenly yanked sideways in its orbit, and the solar system destroyed, with nobody outside Fatima noticing.'

Is this put forward as a serious argument? Surely he will allow that an omnipotent God would be able to control the movements and positions of all the bodies in the universe. On what principle would God be able to give a new position to the sun, or at the very least make it appear to a vast number of people as if the sun were receiving a new position, but unable to maintain the position of the Earth and the planets? Omnipotence means being able to do anything which is not self-contradictory, not being able to work minor miracles that are not too unusual. Professor Dawkins may reply that he is unwilling to consider the possibility of an omnipotent God's existing. In that case, why does he pretend to be examining the miracle of the sun?

A few pages later (p. 104), our author reports a story about Bertrand Russell. Lord Russell was once asked what he would say if he died and found himself being asked by his Creator why he had not believed in Him. He claimed that he would answer, 'There wasn't enough evidence.' Professor Dawkins seems to approve of this reply: in fact, he made it his own in the newspaper interview already mentioned.[12] The natural riposte is surely: 'What evidence would you be willing to accept?' If he is not impressed by so dramatic and well attested a miracle as that of Fatima, what would he count as evidence? Perhaps he would say that he would believe if he saw a miracle with his own eyes. I hope that he would. But from his writing it seems more probable that he would say, 'However unlikely it is that I suffered a hallucination on that occasion when I seemed to see the sun fall from the sky or water change to wine, and however unlikely it is that I have a clear memory of these events even though they did not happen, nevertheless, either of these apparently unlikely things is more likely than that I really did witness a miracle.' If that would be his attitude, then what, so to speak, is God to do?

Faith and free will

Our author ridicules the suggestion (p. 104) that belief could have anything to do with free choice. He writes: 'Believing is not something . . . I can decide to do as an act

---

[12] *The Independent*, December 4th, 2006.

of will.' But in fact, it is precisely the will that distinguishes belief, whether justified or not, from other forms of assent. We can see this in ordinary human affairs. If a husband tells his wife that he will be late home from the office because he has a lot of work to do, why does she believe him? Not because she sees the truth of what he is saying; if she did, she wouldn't need to believe. On the contrary, it is her *good will* towards her husband that causes her spontaneously to accept his explanation for his late return home. If she lacked this good will towards him, she might be inclined to disbelieve him, and perhaps suspect him of going out with his friends.

Again, a pupil in a mathematics class may be told by his teacher that no prime number is the highest prime number, and he may rationally accept this on the teacher's authority, holding by faith something that he cannot demonstrate. Later on, if he learns and understands the argument demonstrating that no prime number is the highest, his knowledge-by-faith will yield to a scientific knowledge. But before he has grasped the proof for himself, his acceptance of the proposition depends on his will. That is, he must have a general willingness to believe what his teacher tells him about maths, provided the teacher doesn't seem to be lying or joking. This is a minimal requirement, but it must be fulfilled. If the pupil were obstreperous or filled with some implacable hostility towards his teacher, it is conceivable that he would refuse to believe the teacher's assertion that there is no highest prime number.

Likewise, the will has its proper place in religious belief. This does not mean, as our author imagines, that religious believers would have to force or hypnotize themselves into believing certain propositions for no good reason. It means, first, that the will of those who are considering the claims of various religions must be upright: set upon truth, rather than on comfort or human approval. If it is not set upon truth, the person's judgement will be distorted.

For example, if serious and competent witnesses tell us about a miracle, such as that of Fatima, or if we see such an event ourselves, the rational conclusion is that God has indeed acted in the world. Yet since we don't actually *see* God acting, it is possible for us, if our will is not upright and desirous of the truth, to deny that He has done so. So if a man resents God, wanting Him not to exist or not to act, it will always be possible for him to say, 'Though I cannot explain what has taken place, I *will* not believe.'

More generally, Catholics hold that if someone has an upright will, then by examining the historical evidence, such as the evidence of the gospels and the evidence of later miracles, he can come rationally to the conclusion, 'the Catholic Church is from God'. Such a person then stands to the Church in something of the relation of the schoolboy mentioned above to his teacher. And just as a sensible schoolboy believes what a properly accredited teacher tells him, so someone who accepts that the Church is the duly accredited messenger of God will be wise to believe her teaching. Even though he doesn't *see* that the doctrines of the Trinity or the Last Judgement are true, he will be wise to accept them, just as the schoolboy will be wise to accept that there is no highest prime number. But precisely because this person doesn't see the truth of the Church's doctrines, he will have to use his will to enable himself to accept them. He knows that it is rational for him to do so, if he has sufficient evidence that the

Church is from God: but he must still choose to do so. Nothing forces him to make this rational acceptance of these doctrines.

So, both in searching to see which religion, if any, is true, and in formally accepting the tenets of a religion, the will has an indispensable role. Its role is not to force us to accept a religion, say Catholicism, in the absence of any good evidence. Its role is to bring us first, to examine the evidence honestly, and secondly, if the evidence leads us to conclude that a properly accredited teacher of religious truth exists, to accept what this teacher says. But to do either of these things, the will must be *good*. That is, the person must have a certain willingness to accept the truth, wherever it leads, even at the cost of sacrifice. Those who lack this preliminary goodwill cannot be convinced by miracles.

Alas, even at Fatima there were men of this kind. One eyewitness tells us that after the sun had been seen to fall from heaven and the air been filled with the cries and supplications of the crowd, some men stood motionless, with their hats still covering their heads, as a sign that they at any rate would give no glory to God.

Chapter 4

PROFESSOR DAWKINS AND THE GOSPELS

Professor Dawkins allots six of his three hundred and seventy four pages to an attack on the gospels as a possible foundation for religious belief (pp. 92-7). His principal claim is that the four gospels give us no reliable information about the life of Jesus Christ, though he is particularly keen to attack their portrayal of Christ's birth. He adds that even if the gospels gave us an accurate portrait of Christ, there would be no reason to believe that He was the Son of God. Let us test his assertions against the facts.

Unwonted deference

First, are the gospels reliable? The high-spirited scorn that our author generally shows for his confreres working in departments of theology yields to a strangely deferential tone when he comes to speak about the four gospels. An imaginary consensus of anonymous scholars is invoked in support of his own sceptical views. 'Ever since the nineteenth century,' we read,

> Scholarly theologians have made an overwhelming case that the gospels are not reliable accounts of what happened in the history of the real world. All were written long after the death of Jesus. (pp. 92-3)

'Although Jesus probably existed,' he magnanimously allows, 'reputable biblical scholars do not in general regard the New Testament . . . as a reliable record of what actually happened in history' (p. 97). 'No one', he claims, 'knows who the four evangelists were, but they almost certainly never met Jesus personally. Much of what they wrote was in no sense an honest attempt at history' (p. 96). He has heard of the theory that some or other of the gospels derived from an earlier written source: rather confusedly he suggests (p. 96) that St Mark's Gospel could be the common ancestor of all four gospels. This is exactly like suggesting that a father might be one of his own children. Apparently on his own authority, since he doesn't now invoke any reputable or scholarly theologians, he affirms that the successive generations of scribes who copied the gospels, 'had their own religious agendas' (p. 93), and by implication changed the gospels accordingly.

Very good. Now let us ask Professor Dawkins a few simple questions.

The transmission of the gospels

First, has he the slightest acquaintance with the science of textual criticism, and with the findings of this discipline in relation to the books of the New Testament? Does he know, for example, that the gospels are immeasurably better attested than any other historical, literary or philosophical work of antiquity? This is true whether we consider the number of surviving manuscripts and papyri, their antiquity, or the independence of their various traditions.

There are vastly more ancient New Testament manuscripts in existence than survive for any secular work.[13] For example, the works of Aristotle are contained in only five surviving manuscripts. The works of the Roman historian Tacitus are somewhat better attested: twenty extant manuscripts contain his writings. By contrast, there are an estimated 5,300 Greek manuscripts containing some or all of the New Testament; some 10,000 Latin manuscripts and 9,300 manuscripts in other ancient languages such as Syriac. Just think what Professor Dawkins would say if the gospels were preserved in as few copies as the works of Aristotle! Yet textual scholars find no difficulty in accepting that these manuscripts contain what Aristotle wrote.

Again, the surviving New Testament manuscripts and papyri are far closer in time to the originals than any other ancient manuscript is to its original. A person unfamiliar with textual criticism might think it a point against the gospels that no complete manuscript of the four gospels is preserved that dates from before, approximately, 325 AD. That this does not in fact cast doubt on the reliability of our gospel texts is shown by the much greater lengths of time that intervene between the writing of other ancient works and the dates of their earliest surviving manuscripts. For example, the historian Tacitus wrote around the year 100 AD. The earliest known manuscript of his work now in existence dates from around 1100 AD, or about 1000 years after he wrote. Again, Aristotle lived in the fourth century BC. The first extant manuscript copy of his work dates from around 1100 AD, some fourteen hundred

---

[13] For more information on this topic, see J. McDowell, *The New Evidence that Demands a Verdict*, Nelson Reference and Electronic Publishing, 1999.

years later. Yet scholars do not doubt that the works of these authors were transmitted accurately through the intervening centuries, even though the vicissitudes of time have destroyed earlier copies of what they wrote.

More importantly, whilst no complete gospel manuscript is known to exist today that dates from before the fourth century, a great number of papyri fragments from, at the latest, the second and third century are still preserved that contain portions of the four gospels. The passages that survive on these fragments agree with the later, more complete manuscripts. For example, the 'Rylands fragment', dated to around 125 AD, is a piece of papyrus carrying a section of the conversation between Jesus Christ and Pontius Pilate from St John Chapter 18, including the words, 'Everyone who is of the truth hears my voice.' Another fragment that has been much discussed of late comes from St Matthew's Gospel. Using sophisticated modern techniques, one scholar has dated it to the first century – though it is fair to add that this dating has not yet won universal acceptance. Is this papyrus hidden away in some inaccessible monastery of Syria or Egypt? No, it is in the library of Magdalen College, Oxford, just a stone's throw from Professor Dawkins.

Again, the gospels are attested by a uniquely varied range of witnesses. For one thing, the manuscript traditions established by scholars are independent of each other, that is, even the oldest manuscripts show minor variations among themselves. This proves that they derive from still earlier copies, now lost. Again, we possess not only the text of the gospels themselves, but also quotations from them in early Christian writers. It has been calculated that from the works of second and third century writers alone it would be possible to verify all but fourteen verses of our New Testament.

In short, serious textual critics do not doubt that the gospels, as written by the four evangelists, have been transmitted reliably to the present day. Sir Frederick Kenyon, a former Director of the British Museum, wrote in his classic study of the question: 'It cannot be too strongly asserted that in substance the text of the Bible is certain. Especially is this the case with the New Testament.'[14] So much for the insinuation that the original text of the gospels has been lost to us through scribal shenanigans.

In reality, it is not supposed scruples about the manuscript tradition of the New Testament that dissuade authors such as Professor Dawkins from accepting the gospels. It is an *a priori* refusal of the possibility of miracles. But as the last chapter showed, such a refusal is a prejudice: that is, a position adopted firmly, yet without sufficient reason.

The authenticity of the gospels

Next question: how does our author explain the process by which four, and only four gospels, supposedly written long after the life of Christ by men who never knew Him, were unanimously recognized as authentic everywhere in the Church? His book gives us no answer to this question, just as it gives us no reason for believing that the evangelists were in fact impostors. With an insouciance surprising in an eminent natural scientist, our author relies on assertions without evidence. Instead of accepting his *logia* on faith, let us weigh the probabilities.

The Church was spread in the years immediately

---

[14] F. Kenyon, *Our Bible and the Ancient Manuscripts*, Eyre & Spottiswoode, 1958, p. 55.

following the crucifixion, as Professor Dawkins cannot deny. By the year 70 AD, say, it was established in a large part of the empire, in such cities as Antioch, Corinth, Alexandria, Rome, Ephesus, Philippi and so on. Those who had known Christ personally on earth would naturally have been held in particular honour by those who had come to believe later through their preaching. The sayings of the apostles, in particular, would have been jealously treasured. How would a man who had never known Christ have been able to write a book, at some point after this date – for this is what our author implies by saying that the gospels were written 'long after' Christ's earthly life – and convinced everyone, in such a great number of churches spread throughout so widely separate cities, that his book was written by an apostle? It would have been morally impossible for such an imposture to succeed. If we put the date of the gospels early, the apostles themselves or their immediate successors would have still been living, and would have pointed out a fraud. If we put the date of the gospels late, the Church would be too widespread for a fraud to be foisted upon it with universal success.

Another question: if the gospels were not written by those by whom they have always been believed to be written, why is there no record at all of their true authors? It is hard for one man to forge a book and not be detected. Is it reasonable to suppose that four different men, writing about the greatest of all subjects and claiming the highest authorities for their writing, should have succeeded in deceiving such numbers of bishops, priests and faithful who had such keen motives to be certain about the authenticity of what was being presented to them? Or again, why did not those pagans who were hostile to the

Church deny the authenticity of the four gospels if there was any room for doubt?

But let us suppose for a moment that the gospels were written after the apostolic age had finished. In that case, their teaching about Christ would either be the same as the teaching already given by the apostles or else it would be different. If it were different – if the apostles, for example, had not preached Christ as the true Son of God – why was no protest raised against what would have been a startling new doctrine? Why were the gospels accepted anywhere, let alone everywhere? But if the teaching of the gospels was the same as that of the apostles, why should the apostles not have been their authors?

We, on our side, have a clear and reasonable account of how the gospels originated. Faith in Jesus Christ as the incarnate Son of God was spread first by the spoken word, not by books. The first preaching of Christ's resurrection was made to the Jews in Judaea by the twelve apostles. Along with the apostles, men such as St Paul, St Barnabas and others carried the message from Judaea to the pagans, into Syria, Cyprus, Asia Minor, Greece, Italy and beyond. The gospels were written so that those who had personally known Christ during His life on earth, and had witnessed His preaching and miracles, might leave a permanent record behind them for subsequent generations. What, in fact, could be more natural?

All the early writers who discuss the question agree that the four gospels came from the apostles and their closest companions. Papias, a bishop in Asia Minor who had personally known the apostle St John, tells us in a book written about 150 AD that the apostle St Matthew wrote one gospel, and that St Peter's 'secretary', a priest called Mark, wrote down St Peter's words as another gospel.[15] St Irenaeus, who was bishop of Lyons in France, and who had been educated by another of St John's disciples, confirms in his book *Against the Heresies*, that St Matthew the Apostle and St Mark the companion of St Peter each wrote a gospel. He also notes that St Luke, the companion of St Paul, wrote down in a book those things that St Paul had preached (the third gospel), and that last of all St John himself, called the beloved disciple, had written his memoirs (the fourth gospel). A contemporary of St Irenaeus, the Syrian author Tatian, wrote a 'harmony of the four gospels'. Yet another second century author, the African Tertullian, speaks of it as a thing accepted by everyone that the Church had received the four gospels from the four men already mentioned. In addition to this early testimony from such varied parts of the world to the apostolic origin of the gospels, still earlier authors, such as St Clement, fourth bishop of Rome, and St Ignatius, bishop in Antioch immediately after the days of the apostles, quote from all four of our gospels.

Professor Dawkins' claim that the four canonical gospels of the Catholic Church were chosen 'more or less arbitrarily' from a dozen or so possible contenders by a 'council of ecclesiastics' is pure fantasy. Historians know of no time when the Church was uncertain which the true

---

[15] Some readers may be surprised that there should be no earlier explicit testimony to the fact that St Matthew wrote the first gospel. In fact, it is not surprising, given the small number of documents that have survived from ancient times until now. Thus the first extant reference to the great Greek historian Thucydides is found in the writings of Cicero, who lived more than three hundred years after his time. Yet no one would seriously doubt the existence of Thucydides, or his authorship of the *Peloponnesian War*.

gospels were. None of the early councils of the Church discussed the question, for there was no need to discuss it. Everyone knew that four gospels had come down from the apostles, just as today everyone knows, for example, that John Milton wrote *Paradise Lost*, even though the work is well over three hundred years old, and very few people will have seen an edition of it produced within a hundred years of Milton's death.

The style and content of the gospels support what the second century writers tell us of their origin. No one, unless perhaps our author, denies that they are written in a first century Greek that contains many 'semitisms', that is, turns of phrase typical of those whose first language was Aramaic (St Luke's Gospel is for the most part an exception, since St Luke was a converted Gentile.) They show a detailed knowledge of the complicated religions and political situation in Palestine in the first half of the first century of our era, a situation that was drastically changed by the destruction of the Jewish temple in 70 AD (incidentally, the first three gospels contain a prophecy of this destruction which would not have been written after the event, since it hardly distinguishes it from the end of the world.) The fourth gospel contains many detailed and vivid touches that give it from start to finish the 'flavour' of an eye-witness account. Its author expressly and solemnly states that he witnessed the crucifixion of Christ.

It was because the gospels came either from the apostles (St Matthew and St John) or from the faithful companions of the two greatest apostles (St Mark and St Luke from St Peter and St Paul respectively), that they were accepted throughout the Church from the earliest times. In denying the authenticity of the gospels, Professor Dawkins is asking us to accept that metaphysical monstrosity, an effect without a cause. The only sufficient explanation of the fact that these four gospels, and only these four, have been received throughout the Church from the earliest times is that given by those such as St Irenaeus who first treat of the subject: they came from men who knew Christ personally. When our author writes (p. 96) that the four gospels have the same status as the mediaeval legends about King Arthur, he is talking the language of fanaticism, not of reason.

The gospel writers are reliable

Professor Dawkins claims that 'Much of what they [the evangelists] wrote was in no sense an honest attempt at history but was simply rehashed from the Old Testament.' It is not clear whether he means that the evangelists were deliberately deceiving their readers by offering them jumbled-up excerpts from the Old Testament under the guise of contemporary history, or whether he thinks that it was only later that readers mistakenly began to read the gospels as historical documents. Perhaps he could not himself say which he means: but either suggestion is wildly implausible.

The charge that the gospels are a 'rehash' of the Old Testament might be more convincing if any of the books of the Old Testament portrayed a man acting with the personal authority of God Himself. This, as will be shown below, is the principal theme of the gospels. Of course, none of the Old Testament books does any such thing. It takes no great specialist knowledge to see that our author's claim is entirely unfounded: in which book of the Old

Testament have the evangelists found that which they supposedly 're-hashed' as, for example, Christ's parables, His exorcisms, the Sermon on the Mount, the calming of the storm, the changing of water into wine, the Bread of Life discourse (Jn 6), the teaching on divorce, the upper room discourse (Jn 14-17), the Passion narratives, the accounts of the resurrection, the description of the Last Judgement (Mt 26)? Of course there are quotations from the Old Testament in the gospels; it would be surprising if there were not, since the Old Testament is full of prophecies of the Messiah who is to come. But I do not see how any honest person who having read the Old Testament turns to the gospels can fail to be struck by the originality of what he finds there.

Does our author think that the four evangelists were deliberately trying to deceive their readers? But if their descriptions of Christ's life were false, it would have been the easiest thing in the world for them to have been refuted. They claimed that Christ had worked miracles on a great scale, and that He had spoken to many people in ways that implied His divine identity. If He had not done these things, if thousands of people had not been publicly and miraculously fed, healed and exorcized as the gospels claimed, Judaea and Galilee would have been full of people able to refute the gospels from their personal knowledge. How, in such conditions, could the Church have struck root in Palestine, to spread from there to the Gentiles?

If the gospel writers were deceivers, they must have been the worst of men. They would have been men shamelessly encouraging others to live for something which they themselves knew to be utterly false. They would have been men corrupt and cynical to an unimaginable degree. How could any man of this kind have created a Personality so original yet so perfect, and combining in so unique a way magnanimity and humility, firmness and gentleness, wisdom and simplicity, as emerges from the pages of our four gospels?

Does our author want to suggest that the evangelists were simply mistaken in what they wrote? Such a suggestion makes no sense. How can one mistakenly suppose that one has been the companion of a Man who healed the sick, raised the dead, told beautiful stories, spoke in a way that only God can speak, prophesied His death on the Cross, and went willingly to meet that death?

Or would he have us believe that no one at the time when the gospels were first written took them to be anything more than a beautiful story, and that only later did people begin to mistake them for historical documents? If so, he has an obligation to suggest a date when he thinks this mistake began. Evidently, he cannot: ever since the time of the apostles, Christians have died for the historical truth of the gospels. The apostles and evangelists themselves were among the first martyrs.

The resurrection

Rather than remaining in generalities, let us consider one particular part of the gospel message: the resurrection. Why, in our author's opinion, did men come to believe in the resurrection of Jesus Christ? It is a striking fact that nowhere in his three hundred and seventy four pages does he even mention this central tenet of Christianity, let alone explain how something so contrary to human experience came to be so widely held. Does he accept that the resurrection and ascension of Jesus of Nazareth was first preached by Christ's own followers? If he doesn't accept this, it is incumbent upon him to say when he thinks the preaching of these doctrines began and why anyone listened to it. After all, if someone were to say that a certain person, whom he himself had never known, had died and risen again and ascended into heaven, without being able to point to any chain of witnesses linking himself to the man in question, who would listen? People would simply laugh at him.

Presumably, however, our author does accept that the preaching of the resurrection began among Christ's contemporaries, since he alleges that 'Christianity was founded by Paul of Tarsus' (p. 37), who preached in the fourth decade of our era. What is Professor Dawkins' opinion of the first preachers of the resurrection? Were they deceivers or deceived? His book doesn't attempt to answer this question. We, on our side, have a coherent story to tell. We claim that the apostles were with Christ before His death, that they saw Him alive after His crucifixion and that they saw Him depart from this world forty days after the resurrection. We claim that they preached all this with the authority that belongs to men who know that they are speaking the truth, that they confirmed their message with miracles, and that in this way the Church spread to many different parts of the Roman Empire in a single generation. This is the story to be found in the Acts of the Apostles, a document that even the most exacting biblical scholars will acknowledge to be a first century record written by a careful historian. What is Professor Dawkins' story?

Did the disciples simply make a mistake when they said

that their dead Master had risen immortal on the third day and ascended on the fortieth? But once again, how could anyone be mistaken about such a thing? I can be mistaken about the day of the week or the honesty of some acquaintance. But how could Christ's disciples have simply been making a mistake when they said that they had seen Him alive again after the crucifixion and later seen Him ascend into heaven? What was the reality which they mistook for all this?

Will our author say, 'Perhaps he didn't really die; or perhaps the man whom they saw on the third day was just an ordinary human being who looked like Christ.' But if Christ didn't really die on the Cross, and so the apostles were mistaken in thinking that He was risen, when did He die? If the apostles had seen Him die later, that would obviously have been the end of their preaching, if they were honest men (the hypothesis that the story of the resurrection was a lie will be examined in a moment). Or did He go away into another country, so that no one saw Him die? In that case, the apostles couldn't have been honestly mistaken when they preached the ascension; they would have been lying. The same arguments refute the suggestion that another man, who looked like Christ, appeared to the apostles from Easter Sunday onwards. This man either stayed among them, in which case he would have grown old and died and then the apostles could not have honestly thought that he was immortal, or else he must have gone somewhere else to grow old and die in secret, in which case the apostles could not have honestly preached that he had ascended in glory.

Were the disciples of Christ suffering from some kind of hallucination? A sick man in a fever may suffer from a hallucination, but who will believe that many people share the same hallucination, and that this should continue over a long period? It's clear from all the earliest accounts of the resurrection, that Christ was preached as having appeared to His followers not once only, but several times, over many weeks. The 'theory' of collective continuous hallucination is quite fantastic. It would require a miracle: but in that case, why not rather believe in the resurrection?

In short, the first preachers of the resurrection cannot have been deceived. Other considerations apart, it is certain that the Jewish authorities in Jerusalem were hostile to the new sect, as it seemed to them. If they had wished to crush it, they would simply have had to produce Christ's body. That they did not, sufficiently indicates that they could not.

Were the first preachers of the resurrection deliberate liars? Did they hide the body of Christ, and then spend the rest of their lives telling people that He had risen? A sceptic who wishes to maintain this position will have to find an adequate motive for such a lie. The preaching of the gospel brought with it no worldly advantage. The apostles seized no land, piled up no gold, gained no political power or social prestige. They took no new wives; rather, they left behind their ordinary domestic security.[16] They faced persecution both from the Jewish authorities in Palestine and from the civil power throughout the empire. According to the Acts of the Apostles, in the years immediately following the Crucifixion, the disciples suffered imprisonment, flogging, stoning and the sword. According to the Roman historian Tacitus, the mass of the people held them in contempt and Nero Caesar had them

---

[16] See Mk 10:29.

burnt to death. Why would even one person, let alone a group of people, face such things for a lie?

Again, let someone pick up a copy of the New Testament and read what he finds. He may encounter many passages that he dislikes or finds incomprehensible, things strange or severe; but he will not, if he is honest, think that these writings proceed from shameless liars. 'God is love, and he who dwells in love dwells in God'; 'If we say we have no sin, we deceive ourselves, and the truth is not in us'; 'We look for a new heaven and a new earth in which righteousness dwells'; 'It is better to suffer for doing well, if such be the will of God, than for doing ill'; 'Let every man be swift to hear, but slow to speak, and slow to anger'; 'The wisdom that is from above is first chaste, then peaceable, modest, full of mercy and good fruits'; 'If I should distribute all my goods to feed the poor, and if I should deliver my body to be burned, and have not charity, it profiteth me nothing'; 'Bless them that persecute you, bless and do not curse.' Are these the words of evil men or of good ones; of mad men or of wise ones? They are the words of St John, St Peter, St James and St Paul, the first preachers of the resurrection.

Once again, we have a clear and coherent story to tell about how the Church came into being, preaching, just as she does today, the bodily resurrection and ascension of Jesus Christ. It includes – of course – miraculous elements, but not moral impossibilities. It is not improbable that men should preach the resurrection of Christ if they had seen Him risen from the dead, nor that others should believe them when they saw what kind of men they were, and how they had, humanly speaking, nothing to gain by their preaching. Our adversary denies our account, but has nothing to put in its place but sneers and insinuations.[17] Let him give a clear account of what he thinks took place between, say, 30 AD and 60 AD, which is roughly the period covered by the Acts of the Apostles. If he can, we will listen to it. But to say, 'It never happened; it must have been a mistake; it was all exaggerated or invented; it was only written down later on; besides, we all know how tricky those old monks were who copied out the texts' – that will not do.

The infancy narratives

If our author is extremely reticent about the resurrection of Christ, he makes up for it by his critique of the accounts of Christ's birth. No doubt he feels himself to be on safer ground here; anyhow, he stakes his entire case for the mendacity or unreliability of the gospels on the alleged contradictions in these accounts. Let us see how well his arguments will stand up.

St Matthew and St Luke both state that Christ was born in Bethlehem, in the south of the Holy Land, but raised in Nazareth in Galilee, in the north. His place of birth had been predicted by the Old Testament prophet, Micah. Professor Dawkins would have us believe, of course, that the evangelists invented Christ's birthplace to fit the prophecy. So far, we shall probably not be surprised by his critique. But what is very curious is his attempt to *prove* that Christ was not, in fact, born in Bethlehem. He quotes the following passage from St John's Gospel: 'Others said,

---

[17] In the newspaper interview already alluded to, he claims that there is no more evidence for Christ's resurrection than for the story of 'Jack and the Beanstalk'. The reader must judge whether this is the language of a rational man.

This is the Christ. But some said, Shall Christ come out of Galilee? Hath not the scripture said, That Christ cometh of the seed of David, and out of the town of Bethlehem, where David was?' (Jn 7:41-2).

St John is supposed by our author to have let the cat out of the bag, and inadvertently exposed his two fellow evangelists, St Matthew and St Luke, as writers of fiction. Unfortunately, in his eagerness to expose the gospels as unreliable, he has not bothered to read the texts properly. Contrary to what he states (p. 93), it is not Christ's *followers* – who might be expected to know where He came from – who complain that He was born in the wrong place to be the Messiah (after all, they would hardly have been His followers if they were denying His messiahship!) It is simply 'some of the multitude' (Jn 7:40), that is some members of the motley crowd that was present in Jerusalem for the feast day (Jn 7:2), which naturally took an interest in the new prophet and healer as the great topic of the moment, but without having more than a cursory knowledge of His background. The whole passage, of course, is ironic. St John is recording one of the reasons that some people gave for not accepting Jesus of Nazareth as the Messiah, namely that He had been born in the wrong place. He doesn't interrupt his narrative to reassure the reader that Jesus had really been born in the right place; he takes it for granted that they already know all about it.

However, not content with finding a contradiction between St John on the one hand and St Matthew and St Luke on the other, our author now claims that these last two evangelists are inconsistent with each other.

> Matthew has Mary and Joseph in Bethlehem all along, moving to Nazareth only long after the birth of Jesus ... Luke, by

> contrast, acknowledges that Mary and Joseph lived in Nazareth
> before Jesus was born. (p. 93)

In fact, St Matthew says nothing of the kind. He tells us nothing about where Mary and Joseph lived before the birth. True, he doesn't say that they lived in Nazareth, but nor does he say that they lived in Bethlehem. Until Christ's birth, he doesn't locate the holy family in any place at all. Our author is simply fabricating his evidence.

What of the claim (p. 95) that the variant genealogies of Christ in St Matthew and St Luke prove the unreliability of the gospels as historical fact? Our author asks if those of us who accept the literal truth of the gospels ever actually read them (p. 94); we in turn might ask if he has ever considered whether the questions that he raises might not have been addressed at some point in Christian history. St Augustine, for example, is generally recognized, not only by his fellow Catholics but by the world at large, as one of the deepest thinkers in the history of our race. Now, he believed in the literal truth of the gospels, and wrote a book called *On the Agreement of the Evangelists* to defend it. In the course of it, he discusses this very question that our author raises as an insuperable objection to the veracity of the gospels. The great Church historian Eusebius of Caesarea did the same in his fourth century work, *Ecclesiastical History.* I don't criticize Professor Dawkins for being unaware of these books: no doubt he is a busy man, with other things to do than read through the works of the Fathers. Still, we might reasonably expect him, before attacking the founding documents of Western civilization as incoherent, to ask if the great men of the past who handed them down to us had anything to say about their alleged contradictions.

On the present question, neither evangelist states that he is giving *all* the generations between Jesus and King David, so we need not worry that St Matthew mentions fewer than St Luke. Jewish custom allowed a genealogy to be given without all the generations being mentioned, as can be seen by comparing the priestly genealogy in 1 Chronicles 6:3-15 with that of Ezra 7:1-5. After all, St Matthew makes it clear that he is choosing a total number of generations, namely forty-two, for some specific, symbolic reason. As for the difference in names, this can be explained, for example, by the requirement of the Jewish law that a surviving brother should marry his elder brother's widow to raise up children for the elder branch of the family. On this hypothesis, St Matthew would have given the physical ancestry of St Joseph, whilst St Luke would have given his legal ancestry. Our author also complains that if Christ was born of a virgin, St Joseph's ancestry is irrelevant and cannot help fulfil the prophecy that the Messiah would be a descendant of King David. In fact, St Joseph's status as legal father of Jesus Christ would have been enough to establish His status as an heir of David, quite apart from the fact that Mary herself was of the Davidic line.

Does it not strike Professor Dawkins that the various reasons he gives for disbelieving the gospels are inconsistent with each other? One moment he is assuring us that the gospels have been tampered with by crafty scribes; the next moment he is claiming to find 'glaring contradictions' (p. 94) within or between them. Does he really think that men who were seeking to establish a religious imposture as fact would not take care to expel blatant inconsistencies from their principal texts?

Next, what of his attempt to impugn the accuracy of St Luke's account of Christ's birth? I'm sorry to have to say it, but here he shows his bad faith. It would be perfectly possible for an honest materialist to say that St Luke's account of a virgin birth must be false since miracles can't happen, and to leave it at that. But our author is so anxious not to leave one stone of Christianity upon another that he attacks not only the evangelist's honesty, but also his historical competence (p. 94). St Luke states that Christ was born during the first census of the entire Roman Empire, and that this was ordered by Augustus Caesar, and organized in Judaea by one Quirinius, during the time of King Herod. Our author alleges that St Luke was badly mistaken about this, since a non-biblical document records that Quirinius organized a census in 6 AD, several years after Herod's death, and that it was only a local census, not an empire-wide one (the phrase 'badly mistaken' is mine: Professor Dawkins' phrase is not fit for quotation.)

Consider how St Luke begins his gospel. He addresses it to an educated pagan desirous of knowing more about the Church in the following terms:

> Forasmuch as many have taken in hand to set forth in order a narration of the things that have been accomplished among us . . . it seemed good to me also, having diligently attained to all things from the beginning, to write to thee in order, most excellent Theophilus.

St Luke, writing around 60 AD or earlier, undertakes to give a careful account of the facts concerning Jesus Christ to someone outside the Church. Is it likely that he would have begun his work by telling Theophilus that during the reign of Augustus Caesar, the first census of the known world had taken place, if both of them knew that it hadn't?

That would immediately have dissuaded Theophilus from believing the rest of the narration. Yet both of them would surely have known if there had been no such census during Augustus' reign, since the first census of the known world would not be something that men would quickly forget.

If St Luke has made the mistake of which our author accuses him, his blunder would be obvious, self-defeating and avoidable. It would be obvious, in that the first readers of his gospel would have known his description of the census to be untrue. It would be self-defeating, since it would have cast such a general doubt over his veracity that the remainder of his gospel would have been disbelieved. And it would be avoidable, because nothing in his infancy narrative 'turns' on the census being universal; St Joseph could just have easily have gone to Bethlehem with his bride if it had been a census of Judaea alone. Yet Professor Dawkins chooses to assume that St Luke, whom a commonsense reading of his gospel and of the Acts of the Apostles shows to be a careful historian, was guilty of this random folly. This is what I mean by 'bad faith'. It would be more reasonable to assume that the accidental fragments of ancient history that have come down to us in extra-biblical sources simply do not record the census mentioned by St Luke. It is, after all, quite possible to harmonize such fragments as we do possess with the gospel record. Thus, Quirinius would have organized a local census of Judaea alone in 6 AD, as secular history records; and he would have been the 'Judaean co-ordinator' of the worldwide census that took place at the time of Christ's birth, during the life of King Herod.

Professor Dawkins, moreover, should not try to have things both ways. He claims that St Luke introduced the census into his gospel, heedless of chronology, simply so that he might have Christ born in Bethlehem; but just a moment before he says that it is 'complete nonsense' to suppose that St Joseph would have returned to his ancestral home to take part in it. In other words, the story of the census is spurious because it accounts for Christ's birth in Bethlehem, and it is spurious because it doesn't account for it! But why does he say that it is nonsense? King David, it's true, lived 1,000 years before St Joseph, but in Jewish law, land and lineage were intimately connected. Simply by belonging to a certain tribe and to a certain clan within that tribe, one was associated with a portion of land. So it would be natural for those who wanted to enrol as members of a particular clan to register in the territory belonging to that clan. And from the prophet Zechariah we can see that the house of David did indeed exist as a distinct clan within Judah even after the line of Davidic kings had ended (Zech 12:7). What's more, there is no reason at all to suppose that St Joseph's family had been living away from Bethlehem for generations, as our author implies; for all we know, he could have grown up in Bethlehem and simply travelled north in search of work. Here again, Professor Dawkins' sense of realities fails him. If it was 'complete nonsense' to suggest that a man in the first century might travel to another town in order to register in a census, might not some of the first century readers of this passage have noticed the nonsense; indeed, might not St Luke himself have noticed it? But in that case, might he not have abstained from writing it?

Finally, it is interesting to note our author's suggestion that the 'glaring contradictions' in the infancy narratives result from the combination of St Matthew's use of the old Jewish prophecies and St Luke's wish to 'press the familiar hot buttons of pagan Hellenistic religions (virgin birth, worship by kings etc)'. The virgin birth is related, of course, by both evangelists; the worship by the three 'kings' is found in St Matthew alone. Our author should check his sources.

The claims of Jesus Christ

St Thomas More, the martyred chancellor of England, once made this wise remark about Jesus Christ: 'Surely, if he were not God, he would be no good man either, since he plainly said he was God.' In other words, since Christ was neither a bad man nor a lunatic, we should accept that He was what He claimed to be: God incarnate.

Professor Dawkins is familiar with some version of this argument (p. 92). He says that there is another possibility, namely that Christ was 'honestly mistaken'. Prudently, from his point of view, he doesn't try to develop this line of thought. To suppose that Jesus Christ was 'honestly mistaken' in thinking that He was God is even less plausible than to suppose that the apostles were honestly mistaken in thinking they had seen Him risen and ascending. Someone can be honestly mistaken about many things, even very important ones. He might be honestly mistaken about his parentage or the prospects of his career. But how, exactly, does one honestly mistake oneself for God? I think the author realizes the difficulties of his own suggestion, because he abandons it immediately in order to adopt another defence, namely, that 'there is no good historical evidence that [Christ] ever thought he was divine'.

We have already seen that the gospels must be accepted as attempts by Christ's first followers to describe the historical facts of His life and ministry.[18] No other explanation can be given of why they were written or why they were accepted throughout the Church. And anyone who reads the four gospels with care will see that they do indeed present Christ as one conscious of His own divinity.

Of course He doesn't begin His preaching by saying, 'I am God'. How could any people, let alone the Jews with their strict monotheism, be ready to grasp without preparation the astonishing mystery that a man, one of their own race, was also the eternal God? If God becomes man, He can hardly be other than a wise man; and a wise man does not preach astonishing truths without preparing his hearers to receive them. This explains, in part, the vast number of miracles that Christ worked on earth. They were a means of preparing those who saw them to receive the truth about His Person. Likewise, when He spoke, Christ revealed His divinity, for the most part, indirectly. He allowed it to be perceived, little by little, by His own disciples and by the crowds. He didn't say directly, 'I am God'; but he said and did such things, and said and did them in such a way, that those who reflected would understand, in their own time, that there was no other explanation of what they had seen and heard.

For example, Professor Dawkins praises the wisdom of Christ's saying, 'The Sabbath was made for man, not man for the Sabbath' (p. 250). But what, according to the three gospels that quote this saying, does He say next? 'The Son of Man is Lord of the Sabbath' (Mt 12:8; Mk 2:28; Lk 6:5). The Lord of the Sabbath can hardly be other than

---

[18] As a Catholic, I hold that the four gospels are inspired and inerrant: but I am describing here the attitude that any objective historian, whether Catholic or not, ought to adopt in their regard.

the one who gave the Sabbath laws to Moses on Mount Sinai. Christ doesn't explicitly identify Himself with God here; yet no other interpretation of His words is possible. Certainly, neither Moses nor any of the prophets would have dreamt of identifying himself as 'Lord of the Sabbath'. It is a divine title. Likewise, no Jew would have dreamt of saying that he, personally, was 'greater than the Temple', the place where God's glory dwelt. Yet Christ lets His hearers understand that this can be said of Him (Mt 12:6).

On the same page, our author professes to be shocked by Christ's telling His disciples that they must be ready to put Him before their affection for their parents, children and spouses. It would indeed be indefensible for any mere human being to say, 'Whoever prefers father or mother to me is not worthy of me', let alone, 'Whoever loses his life for my sake will find it' (Mt 10:37; Mk 9:35). Only God can tell us that we should love Him more than we do our family or even our own lives. What's more, since Christ's disciples did not desert Him when He spoke these words, even though He was offering them no possessions or prestige, they must have seen something in Him which made it reasonable for Him to speak as He did.

Or again, how can any mere man, not a megalomaniac, say that those who suffer persecution on his account are blessed (Mt 5:11)? But if Christ's loveable Personality, which drew such large crowds to follow Him even to the extent that they forgot to eat (Mk 8:2), and the humility with which He accepted His death, rule out the hypothesis of megalomania, we are forced to conclude that Jesus was something more than simply a man.

How can any mere man refer to the angels as *his*? Yet

the gospels present Jesus as doing this, and, even more strikingly, as doing it in passing, as being not the important point at issue (Mt 13:41; Mt 16:27; Mt 24:31; Mt 25:31; Mk 13:27). Again, how could any mere 'Palestinian holy man' put himself on an equality with the giver of the ten commandments? Yet Christ is shown in the New Testament not only as correcting false interpretations of the commandments, as when He reproves the excessive strictness of the Pharisees concerning the Sabbath, but as perfecting and completing the ten commandments themselves. 'You have heard that it was said to the men of old, Do not kill. But I say to you, that whosoever is angry with his brother shall be in danger of the judgement. . . . You have heard that it was said to them of old, Thou shalt not commit adultery. But I say to you, that whosoever shall look on a woman to lust after her, has already committed adultery with her in his heart' (Mt 5:21-22, 27-8). Christ does not contradict what God had revealed as His will in the Old Testament; but He 're-promulgates' the commandments, as having authority to do so.

Again, Jesus is presented by the gospels as working miracles on his own authority. 'There came a leper to him, beseeching him, and kneeling down said to him: If thou wilt, thou canst make me clean. And Jesus having compassion on him, stretched forth his hand; and touching him, saith to him: I will. Be thou made clean' (Mk 1:40-1). Compare this with the way in which the saints of the Old and New Testaments are presented as working miracles: the great Elijah pleads over and again before he can raise the widow of Sarephta's dead son (1 Kings 17:17-22); St Peter, prince of the Apostles, doesn't presume to attempt a miracle on his own authority, but invokes the name of Jesus to heal the crippled beggar (Acts 3:6). Very different is St Mark's account of the calming of the storm: 'And he was in the hinder part of the ship, sleeping upon a pillow; and they awake him, and say to him: Master, doth it not concern thee if we perish? And rising up, he rebuked the wind, and said to the sea: Peace, be still. And the wind ceased, and there was made a great calm' (Mk 4:38-9). Our author may say that he does not believe in any of these stories: still, he ought to admit the difference between the accounts of Christ's miracles and the others mentioned in Scripture. And he has not explained how the apostles – working men, with ordinary common sense and none too quick to believe – got hold of the idea that they had seen such great miracles if none had occurred.

Again, the gospels present Christ as Judge, not in some limited sense, but as judge of all the nations (Mt 25:32). This is a divine title in scripture (e.g. Gen 18:25; Ps 95:13; Eccl 12:14). Even more strikingly, judgement will be made with reference to how men of all times and places treated Him. Only the Palestinian nation, and presumably only some part of it, had ordinary human contact with Christ, and that only for a few years. Yet He says that on the day of judgement He will say to the just, 'As you did it to one of these my least brethren, you did it to me,' and to the wicked, 'As you did it not to one of these least, neither did you do it to me' (Mt 25:40, 45). If Christ were a mere man, this would be senseless.

Again, let our author ponder the parable of the tenants and the vineyard (Mt 21:33-30; Mk 12 1-8; Lk 20:9-15). The Master, representing God, sends various servants, representing the prophets, to gather the fruits of the vineyard. These servants are killed by the wicked tenants, as the prophets were put to death by those to whom they preached. The story continues: 'Therefore, having yet one son, most dear to him; he also sent him unto them last of all, saying: They will reverence my son' (Mk 12:6). This parable would be meaningless if there were not a fundamental difference between Jesus and the great prophets of the past. They were servants of God: He is the beloved Son. Elsewhere, according to both St Matthew and St Luke, Christ speaks as follows: 'All things are delivered to me by my Father. And no one knoweth the Son, but the Father: neither doth any one know the Father, but the Son, and he to whom it shall please the Son to reveal him' (Mt 27; Lk 10:22).

What now remains of our author's assertion that 'The historical evidence that Jesus claimed any sort of divine status is minimal'? Or if He never said or did any of the things that have been quoted so far, how did the evangelists come to suppose that He had?

Again, we read that St Peter, first of the apostles, requires an inspiration from heaven to grasp who Jesus is: 'Simon Peter answered and said: Thou art the Christ, the Son of the living God. And Jesus answering, said to him: Blessed art thou, Simon bar-Jona: because flesh and blood hath not revealed it to thee, but my Father who is in heaven' (Mt 16:16-7). Christ, incidentally, never speaks of 'our Father' when He is talking to the disciples or the crowds about God. The gospels always show Him distinguishing His relation to God from anyone else's; others may become children of God, but He is the Son of God in a unique and incommunicable way.

At His trial, Caiaphas, the high priest who has already

determined on putting Him to death as a matter of political expediency, asks directly, 'Art thou the Christ, the Son of the blessed God?' Jesus replies, 'I am.' Caiaphas then rends his robes, accusing Him of blasphemy, and the council cries out that He deserves death (Mk 14:61-4). If He had been claiming some merely metaphorical sonship, He would surely have protested that they had misunderstood Him, and that no blasphemy had been spoken. That He did not correct them is proof that they had correctly understood His claim to be literally God's Son and to have the very same nature as God the Father.

All the examples I have chosen so far have been taken from the first three gospels, sometimes called the 'synoptic' gospels. Some critics of the Catholic faith claim that it is only the fourth gospel, St John's, that teaches the divinity of Christ. Our examples show this claim to be false. Still, it is true that we find in St John's Gospel some striking assertions of Christ's divinity that are not present in the synoptic gospels. The prologue of this gospel identifies Jesus as the eternal Word through whom all things were made; distinct from, but not created by, the Father. Again, later in this gospel, in answer to the question, 'Thou art not yet fifty years old, and hast thou seen Abraham?', Jesus says, 'Amen, Amen, I say to you, before Abraham was made, I am' (Jn 8:57-9). That this was understood as a claim to divinity is proven by the following verse, where St John notes that on hearing this reply, some people took up stones to throw at Him. In fact, this evangelist explicitly says that the authorities sought to have Christ put to death because of the equality that He claimed with God the Father (Jn 5:18). Shortly before His Passion, Christ made perhaps the most explicit statement of all: 'I and the

Father are one' (Jn 10:30).

But why continue? This is enough to show any reasonable enquirer that Jesus Christ is depicted in all of the gospels as divine: doing things that only God can do, and saying things that only God has a right to say. If He had not done and said such things, why would the evangelists have written that He did?

Summary

Professor Dawkins offers us no coherent explanation of who Jesus Christ was, of why the gospels were written or of why the resurrection was preached and accepted. In fact, he offers us no incoherent answers to these great questions. He ignores them. But where does the evidence point? The apostles had no motive to preach the resurrection unless they believed it, and no motive to believe it unless they had seen Christ risen again. The rational conclusion is that the resurrection truly occurred. Again, the evangelists' witness to Christ makes it clear beyond reasonable doubt that He was a man who went about doing good, who taught with great wisdom, who accepted His death in humility and who spoke of Himself as divine. The rational conclusion is that He was indeed what the Catholic Church believes, God made man. 'Everyone that is of the truth heareth my voice.'

Note

At one point in his book (pp. 202-6), Professor Dawkins seems to be making an effort to explain the origins of Christianity, though in a way that answers none of the questions raised in this chapter. He tells us about a 'religion' that apparently sprang up on the South Pacific island of Tanna in the middle of the twentieth century. It seems that some of the natives were in the habit of attributing preternatural powers to the white governors of the island, because of the abundance of material goods that these men were able to attain from across the seas. A certain white man, called John Frum, is supposed to have exploited the superstitious envy felt by some of these natives, and to have promised them that one day, cargoes would arrive for them alone, and that their rulers would be expelled from the island. This idea became very popular among the islanders, and in 1941, many of them stopped working, and Frum himself became the centre of a kind of 'cult'. Shortly afterwards, before he died, he told them that he would one day return, ushering in a new age when the mountains would fall flat and the valleys be filled, old people regain their youth, and all the natives would have as much as they wanted of everything. Professor Dawkins further tells us that in the 1950s there was a man claiming to be John Frum's high-priest living on the island who tied an electric wire around the waist of an old woman, who would then fall into a trance and talk gibberish. The high priest claimed that this constituted a two-way radio by which he was in contact with his master. We also learn that as late as the 1990s, there was at least one man on the island still awaiting Mr Frum's triumphant return.

'It is fascinating to guess', our author muses, 'that the cult of Christianity almost certainly began in very much the same way, and spread initially at the same high speed.'

Professor Dawkins writes at one point in his book

that the word 'ill-gotten' might have been coined to describe the possessions of the Catholic Church (p. 358). It is tempting to remark that the word 'ludicrous' might have been coined to describe his attempts to discredit Christianity. 'Why should we not believe in the cargo-cult of Tanna', he appears to be saying, 'as readily as in the gospels?' Why not? Quite simply, because, according to our author's summary of the facts, its founder did not show the slightest sign that he was an accredited messenger of God. He works no miracles. He gives no profound new teaching about the nature of God and man. Such 'teaching' as he does give leads to the breakdown of society. If he obtains a following, it is by appealing to his hearers' lower instincts: covetousness, sloth and resentment. He himself evinces no signs of unusual sanctity. His chief representative makes a fool of himself by claiming that an old woman with a piece of wire round her waist is a radio set. And all this is supposed to provide a parallel to the life of Christ and the apostolic preaching! If this is the best Professor Dawkins can do to discredit our faith, I hope he may be invited to speak at every Catholic school in England.

Chapter 5

PROFESSOR DAWKINS AND THE ORIGINS OF MORALITY

It is time to investigate Professor Dawkins' views on morality. This is a point on which he is somewhat sensitive. In his early work, *The Selfish Gene*, he defended the theory according to which conflicts between individual creatures or between different species should be understood in the light of a more fundamental conflict, namely that between different genes. To express this theory, he coined the phrase which was the title of that book. In the current book, he notes that this phrase has given some people the impression that altruism is impossible, and that reality is so to speak, selfish to the core (p. 215). This, he insists, is a misunderstanding, albeit one that was 'with hindsight, foreseeable' [*sic*]. So he now wants to put the record straight, by showing how a Darwinian atheist, without being false to his own principles, can be a morally good man.

The possibility of altruism

First, a warning is in order. Earlier in his book, Professor Dawkins accuses 'dualists', that is, people who accept that mind is independent of matter, of personifying inanimate things at the slightest opportunity (p. 180).[19] In fact, he

---

[19] He says of such people, puzzlingly enough, that they see 'spirits and demons even in waterfalls and clouds'. I know many dualists, but none who

himself commits this error by calling genes 'selfish'. A gene cannot be selfish, just as it cannot be altruistic, since it has no self that it can either indulge or renounce. A gene is not a moral agent at all. It makes no more sense to speak of a selfish gene than to speak of a gene that is a fine, upstanding pillar of society. No doubt the author would protest, if challenged, that he is simply using a metaphor. Unfortunately, the metaphorical and non-metaphorical use of the terms 'selfish' and 'altruistic' constantly jostle each other in these pages, so that the reader is left wondering whether the distinction between them can be clear in the writer's mind.

Even as a metaphor, the term 'selfish' is strangely *unilluminating* as applied to a gene. Here is the explanation that our author furnishes of his usage:

> The logic of Darwinism concludes that the unit in the hierarchy of life that survives and passes through the filter of natural selection will tend to be selfish. The units that survive in the world will be the ones that succeeded in surviving at the expense of the rivals at their own level in the hierarchy. That, precisely, is what selfish means in this context. (p. 215)

Surely the author sees that it is a mere tautology to say that those genes continue to the next generation which are best fitted to continue to the next generation? There is no reason to apply the word 'selfish' here: it is a truth of logic. One might as well say that colours are selfish, since the presence of one colour across any given surface prevents the simultaneous presence there of any other colour.

---

has seen a demon in a waterfall (and even if somebody claimed to have done, how would this be *personifying* the waterfall?).

But these are relatively minor points. Our author's main concern in this chapter is to show that the genes best fitted to survive do not always influence organisms to act in a 'selfish' way. He notes two main ways in which genes, on the contrary, will be replicated in the following generation by influencing organisms to behave in an 'altruistic' way. (I put these terms in quotation marks, since they can literally be applied only to persons. But our author's application of them to brute animals at least does less violence to the language than his application of them to genes.)

First, certain creatures take care of other 'family' members. Our author calls this 'kin altruism'. This is most obvious when a mother looks after her young, but other examples are also found in nature. Among bees, wasps, ants and termites, elder siblings care for younger siblings (p. 216). Because of the close genetic relationship between these 'family' members, this behaviour makes it more likely that the genes of the creature taking care of its kin will survive to the next generation. In other words, a gene may promote 'altruistic' behaviour; but that very 'altruistic' behaviour helps the gene that promoted it to survive, or rather to be copied to the next generation.

There is another way in which a gene that promotes 'altruistic' behaviour will tend thereby to ensure its own replication. This occurs when two organisms reciprocally act for each other's good. Thus, a bee pollinates a flower, which is an 'altruistic' act on its part; but in doing so, it receives from the flower the nectar that it needs. Therefore, the gene in bees that leads them altruistically to pollinate flowers favours the survival of the bee, and so ultimately promotes its own replication. The author designates this as 'reciprocal altruism'.

These are apparently the two *main* ways in which the 'altruistic' behaviour of an organism can favour the replication of the genes that promote it. But the author suggests that there may be at least two other subsidiary ways in which the same thing can occur. By performing 'altruistic' acts, a creature might attain a 'reputation' for altruism, which would lead to its being 'trusted' by other creatures. For example (p. 218), small cleaner fish that have been observed in the act of cleaning the mouths of larger fish are more likely to be chosen by other larger fish to perform this same task than cleaner fish which have not been so observed. Since the smaller fish receive nourishment from cleaning the mouths of the large fish, their genes are more likely to survive if they can in this way gain a 'reputation for altruism'. Secondly, one biologist has suggested (p. 219) that members of a certain species of Arabian bird pass on food to other members of the species as a way of 'proving' their own prosperity, thus drawing the attention of prospective mates, and so increasing their chances of passing on their own genes to offspring.

All these details are fascinating: but what foundation do they lay for morality? Precisely none. Let us grant Professor Dawkins, for the sake of argument, all that he wants. Let us grant that the natural world has been the stage for a lengthy competition between different genes, and that this has had the paradoxical result of favouring 'altruistic' behaviour over 'selfish' behaviour in the organisms to which the genes belong. Let us even grant that the human race developed as the result of this contest in which altruism-promoting genes were the winners. All this would at most explain why human beings have a *tendency* to look after their young or care for their sick. It cannot explain why they have a duty to do these things.

Let us ask Professor Dawkins directly: does he think that we have a duty to be good? Does he think, for example, that parents have a duty to look after their children rather than boiling them in oil? If he thinks that we have no duty to be good or just or merciful or anything else, then he does not believe in morality. Morality is by definition something *binding*: an objective standard by which we must govern our personal impulses and desires. If he believes that no such objective standard exists to which we have a duty to adhere, then he has no right to pass any moral judgements. He cannot say, 'This is wrong' but only, 'I have no desire to do this,' or 'I do not find this course of behaviour attractive,' or again, 'I feel distress when I see someone act in this way.'

In fact, of course, his book is full of the most vehement moral judgements. Teaching children to accept a divine revelation is 'pernicious' (p. 307). Teaching them to believe in hell is 'child-abuse' (p. 318). The doctrine of hell itself is 'obnoxious' (ibid.). The doctrine of vicarious satisfaction for sin is 'vicious' (p. 253). Separating a baptized child from his Jewish parents is a perversion (p. 313). The New Testament is lacking in family values (p. 250). The Old Testament is nasty (*passim*). And so on. Of all such judgements, we can ask the author, 'Do you think that your words are objectively true – or do you just mean that you, personally, and the people with whom you prefer to associate, do not like these things?' The passion with which he expresses his disapprobation suggests that he considers himself to be *right*, and the actions of which he disapproves to be *wrong*. Yet his account of the origins of morality does not even begin to explain what it means for something to be right rather than wrong.

He tells us (p. 220) that during the earliest stage of human existence, 'we lived . . . in discrete roving bands like baboons, partially isolated from neighbouring bands or villages'. For the sake of argument, let it pass. Such circumstances, he says, would have favoured genetic tendencies to altruism. We should have had plenty of opportunities for 'kin altruism', since the members of our own family would probably have been roving in the same band as ourselves. We should also have had many opportunities for 'reciprocal altruism', since we should have tended to meet the same few individuals constantly. Finally, our circumstances would apparently have been ideal for building a reputation for altruism and for advertising our generosity. Those who took advantage of these manifold opportunities for good deeds would have been more successful at replicating their genes than others, since their kin would be more likely to survive; since they themselves would be helped both by those to whom they had done good and by those who knew their reputation; and since they would have been more attractive to potential spouses.

In other words, during our 'pre-history' we evolved the rule-of-thumb, 'be kind to those who are around you'. The genes that promoted such behaviour were, for the reasons just summarized, more successful at replicating themselves than other genes. Nowadays, altruism may not tend to promote the replication of the genes of those who pursue it, since most of us no longer rove about like baboons. Nevertheless, it remains in us as an ingrained habit, a happy relic of simpler times. That is why we have a tendency to be kind to other people. From the biological point of view, altruism is a 'misfiring'; yet even when we know it for what it is, we can still consider it a 'blessed mistake' (p. 221).

Surely Professor Dawkins sees that none of this provides any answer to the question, 'Ought I to be good?' He has told us a story, which some of his readers may find more plausible than others, about the origin of 'altruistic' tendencies in human beings. But he has not explained why anyone ought to follow such tendencies. After all, he also tells us that our prehistoric ancestors would have been 'bad to the point of xenophobia to other groups'. Presumably some of these xenophobic tendencies must remain in their present-day descendants. What reason, then, do we have to restrain xenophobic tendencies and follow altruistic ones? Or is it all just a matter of personal preference?

Perhaps — I hope so — our author will allow that there is a duty to be good. To judge from his book as a whole, he might even be induced to admit some more specific duty. He might allow that we have a duty never to cause unnecessary suffering, or never to believe in anything without a sufficient reason. If he does, he must explain where this duty comes from. It is no use invoking a time when we were supposedly roving around in tightly-knit bands, when doing good helped our genes to flourish. We don't want an explanation of the *tendency* to do such-and-such a thing, but of the *duty* to do it. Without duty, there is no morality.

What is the source of duty?

If there is such a thing as duty, for example, if is right for a parent to educate his children and wrong for him to boil them in oil, there must be a *source of duty*. This cannot be myself: the very notion of duty implies that my choices need to be regulated by some standard external to myself. Can the source of duty simply be the 'consensus of society' at any given time about what is acceptable? To judge from our author's veneration for 'the changing moral *Zeitgeist*' ('the whole wave keeps moving . . . the progressive trend is unmistakeable and it will continue', p. 271), I fear at times this may be his belief. But if so, what confidence can he have that his moral preferences will always be shared by those who set the tone of society? He gives us to understand (p. 263) that he disapproves of incest. How he can be confident that the wave of the moral *Zeitgeist* may not move so far forward that his views on this point will come to seem rather old-fashioned? Or again, should the unthinkable happen, and Catholic morals return, would he be willing to say that people living in a renewed Christendom of, say, the twenty-third century will have a duty to avoid blasphemy and contraception?

In fact, I cannot believe that Professor Dawkins is a moral relativist at heart. The spirit of indignation that infuses his writing is too strong. Yet if he does acknowledge that he has any duties at all, for example, to seek the truth and live by it, or at least not to boil children in oil, and that such duties would still bind him even if no one else in the world believed in them, he must answer the question, 'Where do these duties come from?'

They can only come to us from a personal being. No impersonal force can lay a duty upon us, for the simple reason that no impersonal force can promulgate a law. Only an intelligent, that is, a personal being can promulgate a law. Duty, if its existence be admitted at all, can only be understood as a law binding us to perform certain actions and to avoid others. The existence of such a law in our minds, which we are conscious of not having created for ourselves, points us inescapably towards a law-giver who is distinct from ourselves and from all human society.

Someone might object, 'This law-giver you have in mind is presumably God. But is God Himself subject to any laws? If so, then it seems that He is not in fact the source of duty, since something must have laid these laws upon Him. But if He is subject to no law, then He could have commanded the opposite of what He does command. He might have commanded adultery and idolatry. Would it then have been our duty to commit these things?'

A Catholic philosopher is likely to meet this objection as follows. First, God cannot be subject to any law outside Himself. Not every law-giver can be subject to a law outside himself, for otherwise there would be an infinite regress, making all laws impossible. There must be a first law-giver, whom we call God. Nevertheless, secondly, it does not follow that God could have commanded the opposite of what He does command. The law of God cannot be something that God *has*; it must be what He *is*. If the law of God were something that God had, it would be distinct from Him; but then we could reasonably ask who gave it to Him. In that case, He would no longer be the first law-giver. Since by definition He is the first law-giver, we cannot ask who gave a law to Him. We must therefore say that there is no distinction between God and His Law. Hence, just as God could not have been different from what He is, neither could His Law have been different from what it is. It is not possible that He might have commanded adultery or idolatry, rather than forbidding them, any more than it is possible that He might have been weak rather than almighty.

To prove the same point in a slightly different way: some actions, such as idolatry, by their very nature turn the person who performs them away from God. God, since He is good, cannot desire anyone to turn away from Himself. Therefore, He cannot command such actions. So when God writes on the human heart, or on tablets of stone, that we must not worship strange gods, He is not acting arbitrarily; nor is He acting under external constraint. He is acting according to His own unchangeable nature.

Sapping the foundations

We can understand now why atheism saps the foundations of morality. To say that without God there is no reason to be good is not to say, as our author imagines, that one is only willing to act well in order to be rewarded by God, or to avoid being punished by Him (p. 226). It is to point out that our duty, since it is not brought into existence by our own free choice, must be promulgated by a law-giver outside ourselves; and that to avoid an infinite regress, this law-giver must not be subject to any duty outside Himself, that is, He must be law and wisdom itself. Hence, if one denies that any such law-giver exists, as the atheist does, then even though one may continue to act in a morally good way, at least in certain respects, one has nonetheless destroyed the possibility of moral truth.

Professor Dawkins seems to realize, at least in part, that his explanation of the origin of the human tendency towards altruism is an insufficient basis for moral truth. He imagines an apologist for religion saying to him, 'Wherever the motive to be good comes from, without God there would be no standard for deciding what is good. We could each make up our own definition of the good, and behave accordingly' (p. 231). This is perhaps the most promising moment in the whole book. Our author seems to be almost on the verge of acknowledging a transcendent source of duty, external to our own desires. Unfortunately, he goes off instead at a tangent, and starts to talk about the dispute in moral philosophy between so-called 'deontologists' and 'consequentialists'. The former group, with whom he indicates his disagreement, are said to believe in certain absolute moral principles, such as the wrongness of procured abortion in all circumstances, while the second group 'more pragmatically hold that the wrongness of an action should be judged by its consequences' (p. 233).[20]

Quite apart from the question of how one may know the consequences of an action that one is still deciding whether to perform, the 'consequentialist' position suffers from a fatal weakness. Ultimately, it collapses into the 'absolutist' position. In order to yield any moral obligations, it must rest upon some such principle as 'always perform the action that will have the best consequences / the fewest bad consequences etc'. But this is just as 'absolute' an injunction as 'never seek to kill a human foetus', or 'never commit adultery'. It is true that the 'absolutists' may have many absolute principles, whereas the consequentialist need have only one. But one he must have, if he claims to be enunciating a moral doctrine. If he thinks that consequences determine the

---

[20] Curiously, though he aligns himself with the 'consequentialists' here, in the next chapter he seems to chide Joseph Stalin for holding that 'ends justify means' (p. 273). What is this but a perfect summary of the consequentialist ethic?

morality of an action, he must mean that 'we have a duty to perform the actions that will have certain kinds of consequences'. If he only means, 'my preference is to perform actions that will have certain kinds of consequences', he is no longer speaking the language of morals.

In other words, not even embracing the so-called consequentialist position can save Professor Dawkins from the need for God. We are not saying 'God must exist, because we shouldn't know that adultery was wrong unless He had told us so,' for then he might indeed reply, 'But I don't think that adultery is wrong if its consequences are good.' Rather, as soon as he admits any moral principle at all, anything that it is our duty to do, even if it is something so nebulous as 'to act for the best', then he is faced with the question of how the duty to follow this principle comes to be laid upon him. If he replies that he does not consider that he has any duty to follow this principle, but that he just wants to, then he has a logically coherent position. But he has destroyed morality.

Chapter 6

PROFESSOR DAWKINS AND THE ORIGINS OF RELIGION

An evolutionary puzzle

Why, if religion is irrational and pernicious, is it so widespread? Our author devotes one chapter of his book to this question.[21] As a committed Darwinian, he cannot allow himself the luxury of shrugging his shoulders and saying like Thomas Carlyle, 'men are mostly fools' (not that he would in any case employ so unfeminist an idiom). Professor Dawkins holds, as a first principle, that 'natural selection punishes wastage of time and energy' (p. 164). He names this 'the Darwinian imperative'. The genes that replicate themselves for a future generation are those that promote efficient behaviour, that is, behaviour favouring such replication. Religion, however, seems on the face of things to be a waste of time and energy. Some religions encourage or even enjoin their adherents to accept serious privations, sometimes to the point of martyrdom. They lead men to construct cathedrals, which take a long time to build yet offer no shelter to their builders. The evolutionary scientist is forced to ask himself, 'What is it all for? What is the benefit of religion?' (p. 165).

Our author is dissatisfied with purely psychological explanations of religion. He does not want to be told that

---

[21] 'The Roots of Religion', pp. 163–207.

'religion is consoling' or 'religion satisfies our curiosity about the world' (p. 168). Such explanations do not seem to him sufficiently fundamental. He wants to know why we are susceptible in the first place to a consolation or an explanation that is so irrational. Nor is Professor Dawkins a Marxist: granted that cynical priests and kings may have used religions as a means of subjugating the masses, this still leaves the question of why the masses were so susceptible to this particular form of manipulation (p. 169). Nor will any neurological explanation of religion suffice. Even if it should turn out that some part of the brain was particularly associated with religious activity, the Darwinian will still ask, 'Why did those of our ancestors who had a genetic tendency to grow a god centre [sic] survive to have more grandchildren than rivals who didn't?' (ibid.). Clearly, we are in deep waters.

Might religion benefit its practitioners after the manner of a placebo? Probably not, according to our author. Though there is, apparently, some evidence that 'religious belief protects people from stress-related diseases' (p. 166), this doesn't seem able to account for the 'massively pervasive worldwide phenomenon of religion'. After all, 'religion is a large phenomenon, and it needs a large theory to explain it' (p. 168). Moreover, he doubts whether religion is really good for the nerves. 'It is hard to believe that health is improved by the semi-permanent state of morbid guilt suffered by a Roman Catholic possessed of normal human frailty and less than normal intelligence' (though, as he handsomely continues, 'perhaps it is unfair to single out the Catholics', since all religion is essentially a way of inducing guilt).

Having disposed of these superficial or erroneous

explanations of religion, the author gives us his. It belongs to the discipline known as 'evolutionary psychology': the attempt to explain the mental traits of human beings by their aptitude to promote human survival. However, he does not consider religion itself to be such a trait. His idea is rather that religions are produced by the 'misfiring' of various human traits that are, in the abstract, beneficial.

What this means will become clearer as we examine his explanation in more detail. But before we consider his various proposals for useful traits that could have accidentally brought religion into being, one point should be clearly made. Even if Professor Dawkins were able to show that belief in God was likely to emerge from certain useful human propensities, as distinct from objective evidence, he would have done nothing at all to discredit theism. There is no reason why a proposition should be false because we have a natural inclination to hold it. The fact that a child has a natural and useful propensity to trust its parents does nothing towards showing that its parents are in fact, untrustworthy. Nevertheless, it is worth examining our author's attempts to sketch possible non-rational ancestries for religious belief. It will show, I believe, the degree to which prejudice blunts his own rational powers.

Explaining religion

Professor Dawkins singles out several human characteristics as liable, though genetically useful in themselves, to lead by accident to religious delusion. The first, and apparently the principal one is the child's readiness to believe whatever his elders tell him. In the abstract, this is a useful trait, since as the author remarks, 'more than any other species,

109

we survive by the accumulated experience of previous generations' (p. 174). It promotes the survival of the race, or rather of our genes, that children believe what they are told: therefore, he concludes, if they are told nonsense, they will believe this as well.

Even if this last statement were true – and in fact it is probably harder to convince children than adults of something patently false[22] – still, it would not help to explain the universal tendency towards religion. Granted that children have a natural predisposition to accept whatever their parents tell them, why would this cause their parents to teach them that there is a Creator rather than that there is no Creator? This 'explanation' of religion could just as well be used by a religious believer to explain the existence of atheism. It doesn't explain why belief in God is 'a massively pervasive worldwide phenomenon' whereas atheism is not.

The second trait that is supposed both to have evolved in man to aid survival and to be accidentally favourable towards religion is the 'intentional stance' (p. 181). By this is simply meant our ability to recognize purpose, in the broad sense of the word, in certain creatures around us. For example, if we see a tiger approach us with its mouth open, we don't just observe its colour and shape, but also that it 'intends' to eat us (p. 182). This tendency to attribute purposes to other creatures is a genetically useful trait: in the particular case of the tiger, it leads us to run away rather than to stand still and be eaten.

How is this supposed to lead, by a 'misfiring', to a belief in God? Insofar as one can reconstruct the author's thought

---

[22] For example, that two people of the same sex can marry each other.

from the assertions that he scatters around this part of the book, the argument would seem to run like this:

1. We have evolved the habit of attributing intentions to things, like tigers, that are important to us. (p. 183)
2. The weather and other forces of nature are important to us, so primitive people and children attribute intentions to them. (p. 184)
3. But later people stop attributing intentions to the forces of nature, and so attribute them to something else. (p. 181)
4. So they believe in God. (ibid.)

All this is rather lame. With regard to (1), whilst it is certainly useful to be able to impute intentions to a ravenous tiger, what benefit is conferred by imputing them to inanimate objects that do not in fact possess them? Presumably none: but in that case, why would such a disposition have been produced by the Darwinian imperative? Next, no supporting evidence is offered for (2). I don't believe that any child would, as he claims, 'impute intentions to the weather, to waves and currents, to falling rocks', except perhaps as part of a game. And even if children or 'primitive people' did so, by what principle of evolutionary psychology would they, on ceasing to do this, begin to impute the same intentions to something else, as (3) suggests? Why should an inherited tendency to impute intentions to things that are important to us lead to us imputing intentions to things of which we have no experience? And even if we did this, why in virtue of the inherited tendency that is supposed to govern the whole process, should we impute all these different intentions to one single being, as (4) presumes, and declare this being the Creator of the universe? Professor Dawkins claims to show that theism might be the misfiring of an otherwise useful tendency; in reality, his explanation limps at every step.

Elsewhere he makes another attempt. Children, he tells us, are natural dualists, that is, they believe that there is a difference between mind and matter (p. 180). Could this be because mind and matter are clearly different things? Not at all, insists our author; that is a mere superstition. But it is an evolutionarily useful thing to believe. Precisely why, is never made clear. The author hints (p. 183) that dualism goes along with primitive man's supposed propensity to impute intentions to beings that are important to him. But he doesn't attempt to prove such a connection, and in fact, it appears unprovable, not to say indefensible. Granted that it is useful to recognize when a tiger is hungry, and even granted for the sake of argument that it could somehow be useful to imagine that the wind was angry when it blew very hard, what does this have to do with the philosophical position that our author calls dualism? In order to believe that a tiger desires to eat me, must I believe that the tiger has a spiritual soul that will survive the tiger's death? He tells us (p. 183) that he doesn't want to pursue the question of the relation of dualism to our capacity to recognize the desires of certain animals – why then does he raise it in the first place? The suspicion arises that although he wants to say that dualism is an evolutionarily useful belief, he cannot in fact find an argument for this conclusion.

Yet even if the belief that he calls 'dualism' could be shown to be genetically useful, how would this show that belief in God was genetically useful? Dualism and theism are quite separate positions; it is logically possible to maintain either without the other. Our author writes that if we believe in a spirit inhabiting the body,[23] we can imagine it moving on elsewhere after bodily death, and thus being a pure spirit. True: but the idea of a pure spirit is not the idea of the Creator of the universe. None of his talk about 'dualism' and 'teleology' and 'the intentional stance' comes close to establishing the point for which he is arguing, namely that the belief in a Creator is likely to result as an irrational by-product of human characteristics that are in other respects useful.

Let me repeat at this point that even if Professor Dawkins' attempts to show that religious belief could emerge as the misfiring of otherwise useful traits were successful, religious believers need not be bothered in the slightest. To show that a belief could emerge in some non-rational way is not to show that it must do so. It is not to show that it could not also emerge in perfectly rational ways. If our author's arguments were sound, they would not have the least tendency to undermine the rational arguments for God's existence that we have already discussed. But in fact they are unsound.

A little further on (p. 187), he suggests that the tendency to have irrationally strong convictions is also evolutionarily useful, and therefore another possible explanation for belief in God. The fickle man achieves nothing, whilst the man who persists in a course of action upon which he has once determined, will sometimes at least be successful. Should this second kind of man adopt irrational beliefs,

---

[23] Contrary to the author's claim (p. 180), those who accept the position that he calls dualism, need not believe that the spirit merely 'inhabits' the body, like a man inhabiting a house. No orthodox Christian believes this. Body and soul compose a single substance, even though the soul survives bodily death.

he will be likely to persist in them, even in the absence of good evidence; thus religion is born.

Once again, the reasoning appears simply childish. Granted that stubbornness may sometimes be a more beneficial character trait than fickleness, why should not reasonableness be better than either? But then why did the evolutionary process in which our author believes not produce this most desirable quality? Yet let us grant for argument's sake that stubbornness is a more genetically useful trait than reasonableness. Why should stubbornness tend to produce a widespread conviction of the existence of God, rather than of His non-existence? Professor Dawkins' 'explanation' simply amounts to saying, 'men are religious because they tend to persist in the philosophy of life that they have once adopted', when the whole question at issue is why so many people adopt some kind of theism as their philosophy of life. From a man whom the dust-jacket of his book proclaims as 'one of the world's top three intellectuals',[24] and 'the author of many classic works on philosophy',[25] one might have expected something a little more rigorous.

The logical vice of assuming what one needs to prove is ubiquitous in this chapter. It is evolutionarily useful, our author writes, to be able to deceive ourselves, since this allows us the better to deceive others. The conscious liar looks shifty and so is disbelieved. The unconscious liar looks sincere; he has deceived himself so well that he can convince others. Let it be so: how does this lead to theism rather than to atheism? St Paul tells us that atheists 'keep the truth about God captive' (Rom 1:18). Why should it not be the atheists who have

---

[24] According to a vote organized by *Prospect* magazine.
[25] The works are not named.

deceived themselves, the better to deceive others? Once more, our author's arguments which would, I repeat again, be harmless even if sound, are unsound: mere assertions, resting on nothing, leading nowhere.

Finally, on p. 188, we are told that religion is mere 'wishful thinking'. By this point, the author seems to have forgotten his original intention, since he offers not even a weak reason for supposing that wishful thinking would have been evolutionarily useful. He also seems to have forgotten that twenty pages earlier he quoted, with approval, an American comedian who claimed that religion exists to produce guilt. Why would 'wishful thinking' manufacture something so unpleasant? Or why would judgement and the punishment of sin loom so large in so many religions? Our author cannot decide with which stick he wants to beat religion: as a result, his arguments cancel each other out.

Our conclusion must be that the attempt to show that religion would naturally arise from non-rational forces is an entire failure. Not only are the author's arguments extremely muddled, so that it is difficult to see where one ends and another begins, when they are with difficulty brought to light they are seen to rest on untrustworthy foundations, or not to lead to the desired conclusion, or both. Professor Dawkins is the Charles Simonyi Professor for the Public Understanding of Science at Oxford University. This chapter lets the public understand that evolutionary psychology, as practised by our author, is about as much a science as reading tea-leaves.

Sawing off the branch

Our author, as we have seen, considers himself subject to the 'Darwinian imperative'. He holds that all the capacities of living things as such are the result of evolution. He also holds that evolution is driven without any transcendent purpose: a given gene simply replicates itself if it is in a position to do so, and fails to replicate itself if it is not. He exults in the supposed explanatory power of this 'imperative'. But he doesn't seem to realize what a hard taskmaster it is.

If all human powers are a result of a blind process of evolution, then our capacity for making judgements is also a product of this blind process. Our minds, which according to Professor Dawkins are simply an aspect of our bodies, must have evolved those powers most favourable to the continued existence of our genes. In other words, the principle that fundamentally governs the working of our minds is utility. Just as, according to the Darwinian, man has developed the lungs that will best help him to breathe in the particular atmosphere that is the earth's, so also has he developed the minds that will, accidental 'misfirings' aside, best promote survival.

But if this were so, we should have no reason to be confident that our minds could grasp the truth. If the ultimate principle that directs our thinking is utility, we shall have a tendency to believe what it is most useful to our genes that we should believe, but not necessarily what is true. Nor is there any reason to suppose that these two things must coincide: it would no doubt be useful to our genes that every person should believe that he or she had a duty to have as many children as possible, but that does not make this belief true.

Our author may protest, as he does in another context (p. 222), that Darwinism does not imply determinism. Though I have a tendency to believe whatever will be most useful to the survival of my genes, still, I can correct this tendency by education. But such an answer is not logically permissible to a Darwinian of the strict observance like our author. If the very nature and intrinsic bias of the mind is towards useful beliefs, as the Darwinian imperative insists, then whatever education we receive, the mind will never be able to step outside itself and judge its own beliefs according to a standard other than that of utility. If both your hands shake, you cannot use one to hold the other still. If the governing principle of our judgement is utility, we cannot judge our own judgements by a principle independent of utility, such as truth.

In other words, the materialistic Darwinism professed by our author is a self-refuting system. It claims to tell us the truth about all living things, including the intellectual animals that we are. But by claiming that we have evolved minds whose property is to assent to useful beliefs rather than to true ones, it takes away our assurance that our minds are in contact with reality. If the assent of our minds is governed by what is useful and not by what is true, we cannot even be confident that $2 + 2 = 4$. Much less can we be confident of the truth of some great philosophical system, such as Darwinism.

Darwinism is thus in practice a form of relativism. It denies, not explicitly but in virtue of its own logic, that our minds were made for a truth independent of ourselves. But the relativist, whatever label he may wear, infallibly cuts off the branch on which he sits. He professes a doctrine that would render all doctrines, and therefore his own, valueless. Like the heretic of whom St Paul warns St Titus, he is self-condemned (Tit 3:11).

Chapter 7

PROFESSOR DAWKINS, MORALS AND THE BIBLE

A significant part of Professor Dawkins' case against religion is ethical.[26] He holds that the principal religions of the world are not only irrational, but also immoral. They urge their adherents to do things that go against ordinary, human decency. He quotes with approval a dictum of Blaise Pascal (himself, of course, a convinced and even fervent Catholic), 'Men never do evil so completely and cheerfully as when they do it from religious conviction.'

Now, it is not my purpose in this book to defend 'religion' in general against the author's onslaught. I write as a Catholic, not as a 'pan-religious apologist'. I also believe that some religions, though not my own, teach or foster immoral doctrines. Still, one point is worth making in answer to the author's claim, as old as Lucretius (and no doubt much older), that 'religion causes people to do evil things'. Insofar as this is true, it has no tendency to show that religion is itself a bad thing, or that its message is false. Love causes people to do evil things; so does patriotism. The love of a man and a woman can lead to unfaithfulness, to the destruction of families and even to murder. Patriotism can lead to hatred and to the

---

[26] Chapters 7 and 8 of his book.

indiscriminate bombing of cities. None of this means that either love or patriotism is a bad thing. It simply means that the weakness of human nature is such that any great object or cause may so stir our emotions as to lead us to act against our better judgement. If religion occasions evil as well as good, this is no sign of its falsity, but simply of its power of attraction over human nature. That in the name of religion good men may do bad things is no argument against religion, unless crimes of passion are arguments against human love.

Nor shall we allow Professor Dawkins his further claim that since atheism, unlike religion, is a mere 'absence of belief', it is impossible that anyone should do evil in its name (p. 278). Atheism is not a mere absence. It is a philosophy of life. Like the various religions, it too sets up its ideal, one that can be seductive to human weakness: 'man without God / man come of age / man the master of his fate etc'. Like the various religious ideals, this also has a power to stir up human passions: let him think of the French revolutionaries, and their guillotines.

Or let him think again of his own example, Joseph Stalin. The author would have us believe that while Stalin was both an atheist and a tyrant, it was never in the name of atheism that he oppressed his subjects. Stalin, he tells us, was simply motivated by 'dogmatic and doctrinaire Marxism' (p. 278). But is not atheism one of the principal dogmas of Marxism? And does he really think that the ruthlessness of Stalin and his comrades was exercised only for economic ends – to provide free cabbages for all? Surely they too had some guiding 'inspiration', a vision of Man without God building the perfect State. Why else does he think they closed down the churches, and shot or jailed so many priests and bishops?[27]

No doubt atheists need not be Marxists. But it is an historical fact that where atheism has been established as the official doctrine of a State, whether in Soviet Russia or Maoist China, the result has been oppression and misery on an inconceivable scale. That might at least give our author pause.

But if it comforts him to think that no one has ever done evil in the name of atheism, let him think so. We can wait until the Day of Judgement, after all. In this chapter I simply want to compare two rival moralities: his and ours.

Creature and Creator

The gap between the atheistic and the Catholic view of reality is such that it is difficult to know where to begin in answering Professor Dawkins' charges. This is not to say that no common, ethical standard is possible for believer and non-believer. On the contrary, the Catholic Church, following St Paul, insists on the reality and binding force of natural law, inscribed by God in the heart of every human being. When our author notes that people of all religions or none tend to give the same answers to certain moral problems to do with the saving of human life (pp. 222-6), he is not, whatever he thinks, making a point against the Church, but rather illustrating this very doctrine. Instead, then, of concluding with the author that 'we do not need God in order to be good' (p. 226), the Catholic will conclude that the denial of God's existence

---

[27] We can think, for example, of Stalin's wholesale persecution of Catholics in Romania and the Ukraine.

can co-exist with some correct moral judgements, because of the (God-given) law inscribed on our hearts. Nevertheless, as mentioned in a previous chapter, the man who denies God's existence cannot logically ascribe a binding force to his moral judgements, even when he acts from a conviction that they are indeed binding.

No, the real difficulty in answering a writer such as Professor Dawkins is his lack of a sense of sin. So at one point we encounter the following outburst:

> The Christian focus is overwhelmingly on sin sin sin sin sin sin sin. What a nasty little preoccupation to have dominating your life. (p. 252)

According to the dust-jacket of his book, our author is a Fellow of the Royal Society of Literature and a past recipient of the Shakespeare Prize. I shan't presume, therefore, to criticize his prose style: but his attitude certainly makes it difficult for anyone to explain the Old Testament to him.

It's not that he has no appreciation for any of the virtues. He admires, for example, the honesty of scientists who publicly abandon their cherished theories when confronted with contrary evidence (pp. 283-4). Elsewhere he praises the late Cardinal Hume as 'saintly' (p. 358), though how anyone can be saintly if there is no God to sanctify him is a problem that he apparently doesn't notice.[28] But he does not care to understand what the Church means by saying that sin is an 'offence against God'. It is not simply that he doesn't accept this definition of wrongdoing. He doesn't see that

---

[28] On the other hand, it is sad to see the invective which he reserves for Mother Teresa of Calcutta (p. 292). How anyone can contemplate her life except with humility and admiration is beyond me.

it follows necessarily from the Church's doctrine of God as the transcendent Creator who alone exists of Himself. We hold that the badness of a bad deed consists not primarily in any harm that it does to other people, or even to the man who commits it, but simply in being a revolt against God: a rebellion against the Love that created all things.

In fact, the author has little sense of what Christianity means by creation *ex nihilo*. The explanation that he gives of deism and theism (pp. 18, 38) shows this clearly enough. The distinction, or rather chasm, between these two positions is not simply that the 'God of theists' acts in the universe while the 'God of deists' (in whom, I suspect, no one has ever believed) does not so act. It is rather that according to orthodox Christianity, against which the eighteenth century 'deists' were in revolt, God did not simply fashion the universe at some time in the past out of pre-existing matter: He holds it in being at each moment. As the *Catechism of the Council of Trent* puts it, 'Unless preserved by the same power that produced them, all things would instantly return into nothingness.' That is what is meant by a Creator: that, incidentally, is why it makes no difference to the need for a Creator whether the universe had any beginning in time or not.

Professor Dawkins does not only not hold this doctrine of creation; he does not even seem to understand it. The most that he attributes to the Christian God is a power 'to oversee and influence the subsequent fate' of creation (p. 18). Lacking, even to deny it, the notion of a transcendent Creator on whom we depend at every moment, he inevitably conceives of God as a finite 'moral agent', more powerful than mankind, but otherwise bound by the same rules of behaviour as men. This is what gives his remarks on biblical morality their general air of futility, quite apart from the individual blasphemies which he scatters over his pages. He does not see that the fact of creation must give God *rights* over His creatures immeasurably different from those that any human being could have over any other. This does not mean, as we have seen, that God could command anything at all. He could never command us, for example, to hate each other, to desire another's eternal damnation, to disbelieve His promises or to practise idolatry. Any of these things would contradict His nature. But it means that He has the rights of life and death over every human being, for what He freely gives, namely existence itself, He has the right freely to withdraw. When once we have understood this, the author's objections to the Old Testament fade away like dreams in the light of day.

Professor Dawkins and the Old Testament

So we read (p. 238) that 'The moral of the story of Noah is appalling.' So little does our author care to enter into the mind of the believer, that he doesn't bother to argue his case. Perhaps he means that we human beings do not think it right to drown those of whom we disapprove; therefore it cannot be right for God to have sent a flood to punish sinners. But anyone who so much as understands the Church's creed, whether he accepts it or not, will simply laugh at this. God's relation to mankind is not comparable to our relations to each other. Just as He gives us existence without our having done anything to deserve it, and preserves us in being at every moment, so He can without injustice bring our lives to an end at the moment He sees best, whether by natural or miraculous means. And since He has inscribed the moral law on our hearts, He has the right to judge our behaviour, and to reward or punish it as it deserves.

Our author, however, cannot understand why God should want to judge us. 'Why should a divine being,' he writes, 'with creation and eternity on his mind [*sic*] care . . . for petty human malefactions?' (ibid.). Again, this shows a simple ignorance of what we mean by God and by sin. God is infinite, uncreated goodness. Therefore He has the right to be loved and obeyed unconditionally. This is simply how things are. God can no more abolish His rational creatures' duty of obedience and love towards Him than He can abolish the laws of mathematics. Sin is a refusal of God's right to be loved and obeyed. It is a metaphysical monstrosity: a created will trying to raise itself above the Will that created it. God owes it to His own goodness and holiness not to ignore sin, for that would be to allow evil to subject Him to itself. He can forgive sin on condition of repentance, or He can punish it, but He cannot pretend that it is insignificant, any more than He can cease to be God.

Next, the author objects to the biblical account of Abraham and Isaac (pp. 242-3). How could God test Abraham by asking him to sacrifice his only son? Once more, none of us can have any claims against God, since all that we have, we hold only by His good pleasure. We have no right to go on living beyond the moment that He assigns for our death. If God had willed that Isaac's life in this world had reached its proper term, then He had the right to end it. It is as simple as that. And if, in an entirely exceptional manner, He should make known His will that another human being, such as Abraham, should be the means of bringing Isaac's life to an end, then this other human being would have the duty to accept this. This would not be murder, for to murder is to take another's life unjustly, and it cannot be unjust for God, whether acting directly or by means of an instrument, to take a life that He has bestowed for a period known to Himself alone.[29]

Our author wants to know how Isaac could have been expected to recover from the 'psychological trauma' of the events of Mount Moriah. One is rather reluctant to offer any answer, partly for fear of trespassing on the simplicity of the biblical account, partly because Professor Dawkins, schooled (alas) by 'progressive theologians', doesn't believe that these events happened anyway. Nevertheless, lest he should think us unable to reply, we can give the following answer. First, Isaac was not a small boy when these events took place. According to the chronology of the Douai version of the Bible, he would have been twenty-six or twenty-seven years old. Secondly, we are surely not to imagine that his father suddenly seized him without explanation. Abraham would have explained to his son what God had asked him to do. And incredible though it may seem to our author, I believe that his son would have accepted. The history of the Church contains examples of martyrs younger than Isaac who have been willing to give up their lives rather than disobey God's commands.

But there's little point in answering each of our author's objections to the morals of the Bible. If one accepts that God has the rights of the Creator over the creature and that sin is a monstrosity that He owes it to Himself not to condone, then one will be able to accept the teaching of

---

[29] We also hold that there is a profounder meaning in this story than appears on the surface: Isaac, the sacrificial victim, is restored alive to his father to foreshadow the resurrection of Jesus Christ.

the Old Testament. If one does not, then one will not. Some of Professor Dawkins' objections are in any case beside the point. He mentions the story of Jephthah (p. 243), whom he supposes to have offered his daughter in sacrifice. In fact, the meaning of the passage is uncertain: it is quite possible, given that her companions specifically bewail her virginity, that she was simply offered to God by a life of perpetual continence (Judg 11:37-8). But even if he had taken her life, nothing in the Bible says that this would have been a good deed or pleasing to God: St Jerome and St Thomas Aquinas, who both assume that her life was taken, say that the action was bad. Again, what point, exactly, does Professor Dawkins think he is making when he rehearses the story of the Levite and his 'concubine' from Judges 19? Simply because the Bible does not explicitly condemn an action, in this case, the concubine's being offered to the townsfolk, does he suppose that it must be condoning it? That would be naïve: it's not the manner of Scripture to interrupt its narration at every moment with moral judgements. As for the Levite's dismembering of the dead body, an action on which the Bible again passes no comment, is it not obvious that this is done precisely to awaken the whole nation to the horror of what has occurred?

As a little light relief, we may notice the author's suggestion (p. 241) that the resemblances between this story of the Levite and that of Lot entertaining the angels may indicate that 'a fragment of manuscript became accidentally misplaced in some long-forgotten scriptorium', and that this would be an illustration of his theory of 'the erratic provenance of sacred texts'. Does inventing facts to support one's theories really count as the scientific method?[30]

Next, it is not true, as our author claims (pp. 253ff) that the Bible promotes hatred for those who do not belong to the religious 'in-group'. True, Joshua is commanded to destroy certain specified tribes inhabiting the Promised Land. We learn from other passages of the Bible (Leviticus 18, Wisdom 12) that this was a punishment for the appalling practices of these tribes, including cannibalism, bestiality, incest, and burning their children to death in honour of the devil; and that even here God gave these Canaanites many chances to repent before the sons of Israel arrived to execute His judgement upon them.[31] But thereafter, the Law lays down that the Israelites are to treat any foreigners who may be among them with justice and generosity. They are not to 'molest' any foreigner, for they were foreigners in Egypt, and they 'know the heart' of a stranger (Ex 22:21, 23:9). More than this, God commands the Hebrews: 'the stranger who sojourns among you shall be to you as the native among you, and you shall love him as yourself, for you were strangers in Egypt' (Lev 19:34). The foreigner has the same right to due legal process as

---

[30] As if in any case the whole point of the stories were not different, the abuse occurring in one and being miraculously prevented in the other.

[31] Contrary to the general law laid down in the Old Testament for warfare, the children of these tribes were also to be killed. (Deut. 20:10-18). Clearly, infants would have been innocent of the crimes committed by their parents: but the lives that they had from God could be justly ended by Him. Presumably, one reason why God ordained that this should be done was that in the absence of their parents, the infants would have had no one to raise them. The souls of these infants would have survived death; and Catholic theologians hold that such souls enter a state of untroubled happiness, even if they do not enter heaven.

the Israelite (Lev 24:22). He is to be invited to 'make merry' with the Israelites on their feast days (Deut 16:14). If he is poor, he must be paid his wages each day before sunset (Deut 24:14). When the Israelites are reaping their corn or harvesting grapes and olives, they must not return to collect what they left behind the first time: they must leave it as a gift for the foreigner and for others in need (Deut 24:19-22). All these commandments are taken from the Law of Moses. They show the utter falsity of our author's claim that the Old Testament teaches systematic hostility towards non-Jews.[32] As for his assertion (p. 257) that Jesus Christ taught hostility towards non-Jews, has he ever heard of the parable of the Good Samaritan?

Finally, Professor Dawkins wishes to know why those who believe that Holy Scripture is inspired by God do not seek to put all its provisions into force in modern society, demanding for example that adulterers be stoned to death. But surely he has heard of the Christian belief that the Old Law was given only for a time, namely until the coming of the Messiah to whom the Law pointed? True, the Old Testament's condemnation of certain acts, such as the capital offences which he quotes from the Book of Leviticus (p. 248), remains forever valid. But this does not mean that the specific penalties that were assigned for those offences at that time and among that people need be enacted today by Christian rulers. To curse one's father or mother is as sinful now as in the time of Moses, but it does not follow that Christian courts must order transgressors of this kind to be stoned to death. Old Testament Israel was meant to be a sign to the gentiles of the holiness of God; no

---

[32] The quotation (p. 254) from Moses Maïmonides is not to the point, since he was a mediaeval rabbi, not a biblical writer.

civil society today has this vocation. Therefore, certain sins which were capital offences under Old Testament law need not be treated so severely by the civil magistrate in other societies. One may add that certain acts can become so widespread in a society, especially one that has renounced God, that legislators will be unable to root them out even if they desire to.

What is a good action?

Professor Dawkins, then, dislikes the morals of the Bible. What does he propose to put in their place? Insofar as he has any general principle to offer, it seems to be that suffering is the worst of all evils. So, speaking of abortion, he suggests that the proper question to ask is not, 'is the embryo human?' – as a teacher of biology, he knows perfectly well that it is – but, 'is it capable of suffering?' (p. 298). In the same place, he goes so far as to imply, although holds back from positively stating, that an adult pig or cow is of more value than a newly conceived human being, since it can suffer more.

Happily, our author is not perfectly consistent with himself. His spontaneous moral judgements are better, sometimes, than his principles. Faced with a more safely hypothetical question than that of abortion, namely whether it is legitimate to push one man off a bridge onto a runaway 'train-trolley' in order to save the lives of five others, he becomes a moral absolutist. 'Almost everyone agrees that it is immoral' to do this, he writes: and 'almost everyone' seems meant to include himself (p. 223). Very good: but how can this be reconciled with the insistence that abortion is legitimate when it leads to less suffering than pregnancy and birth? Surely, in the hypothetical case of the runaway trolley, the best way to reduce suffering is to push one man off the bridge to save the five others? Yet the author writes that 'most of us have a strong intuition' that it would be wrong to kill this innocent man to save five. Minimizing suffering, therefore, cannot be the criterion of moral action. So how does it justify abortion?

Perhaps he might reply: the man on the bridge has more capacity to suffer pain than the foetus. Quite possibly (although not if he is drugged and unconscious); but the five people who will die if he is not pushed all have a capacity to suffer equal to his. If it is wrong to take away his life even though this will prevent so much suffering, 'preventing suffering' need not make an action good. What then is a good action? The Catholic will say that it is an action in accordance with the law of God, a law written on our hearts and confirmed by revelation. What will the secularist say? If we are to judge by Professor Dawkins, he will say that he does not know.

Professor Dawkins' four commandments

Lacking any coherent views on morality, will our author simply tell everyone to do what he wants? Not exactly. He is by temperament a proselytiser: the absence of a consistent creed will not stop him seeking converts. Nor will his outrage at the notion that his Creator might tell him to do something prevent him from promulgating commandments for his fellow men (p. 264). Yet here as elsewhere his remarks have a curiously slapdash air – he speaks of 'my amended Ten Commandments', but only gets as far as positively assuming responsibility for four. When a legislator is so uninterested in his own laws, why should anyone else bother about them? Still, he does promulgate four. Let us consider them, and see what society would be like if Professor Dawkins were in charge of it.

The first commandment is an exhortation to complete sexual licence, 'so long as it damages nobody'. The second is 'Do not discriminate on the basis of sex, race, or (as far as possible) species.' The third is 'Do not indoctrinate your children: teach them how to think for themselves, how to evaluate evidence and how to disagree with you.' The fourth is 'Value the future on a timescale longer than your own.' This is the 'new law' of Professor Dawkins. What is it worth?

Commandment 1. It seems best to say, simply, that if anyone thinks such licence can be practised 'without damage' to human happiness, character or honour, he must be living in a dream world.

Commandment 2. What on earth does this mean? Professor Dawkins solemnly commands us not to discriminate, 'as far as possible', between species. A cabbage presumably belongs to a species. Does he mean that we should be no more willing to eat cabbages than to eat people? Or that we should be as willing to eat people as to eat cabbages? Either choice would be possible: and he expressly tells us not to discriminate between species except when this becomes impossible.

Or again, most countries have universal suffrage. According to Professor Dawkins, must we therefore also give the vote to orang-utans? Or to gerbils, or geraniums? In fairness, that would not be so possible. But again, bacteria must belong to some species or other. It would be quite possible not to discriminate against them as we currently do by using antibiotics to save human life. Is this really what he is, not just suggesting, but commanding us to do? Or what if a dog attacks a baby? Would it be wrong to shoot the dog to save the baby's life? It would certainly be possible to stand back and do nothing, discriminating against neither the baby nor the dog.... I hope that our author was simply not thinking very much when he laid down this commandment for posterity.

Commandment 3. I suppose that many parents, especially of teenagers, may be amused by the notion that their children need to be taught to disagree with them. More seriously, and setting aside the first part of this commandment (which is, of course, code for 'do not teach religion to your children'), one could in the abstract approve of these sentiments. Only, our author has no right to them: we saw when discussing the 'Darwinian imperative' that if the human mind is only the product of a battle between genes, any or all of our judgements may be mere genetically useful delusions. How then can we urge anyone to teach, or anyone to learn?

Commandment 4. At last, we can agree. 'Time is short, eternity is long.'

Great leaps forward

Our author makes a final attempt to prove the superiority of secular morals over Christian ones by describing what he takes to be the moral progress made by much of the human race in the course of the twentieth century (pp. 263-72). He argues that there has been a moral advance, and that Christianity has not contributed to it. The trouble with this is that the author himself fixes the moral standards according to which he asks us to assess the evidence. He decides for himself what is to count as moral progress or moral decline, and then demands that we praise the twentieth century for providing examples of the one rather than the other. But, of course, it is precisely the author's moral standards that a Catholic, for example, will reject. Either we shall not agree with Professor Dawkins about good and evil, or else we shall not attach to certain changes the importance that he does.

For example, it is no doubt a good thing, in a rather mild way, if offhand abusive nicknames for members of other countries are less common today in this country than in the past (pp. 266, 269). But some would consider this form of 'self-censorship' rather a poor exchange for the massive growth in the media of, say, sexually explicit material. In any case, it is very doubtful that the change of which he approves really indicates a widespread increase of benevolence. It seems more likely that it arose naturally from the unprecedented level of immigration after the Second World War. Reasonable people avoid language likely to give needless pain to their neighbours; they always have done. If the ethnic background of their neighbours changes significantly, their language will therefore also change. This is simply the application in new circumstances of an existing moral principle: it is not a dramatic growth in virtue.

Again, the author thinks it a clear sign of the moral superiority of the twentieth century over its predecessors that 'all civilized nations' have given women the right to vote in general elections (p. 265). Others, however, will think that the right to put a cross on a ballot-paper every four or five years is worth very little in comparison to a happy family life. Yet the same century which promoted female suffrage also destroyed the sanctity of the marriage bond. Progress or decline?[33]

Again, our author takes it to be a sign of moral improvement that it is now less socially acceptable to shoot wild African animals for sport (p. 268). Maybe it is; but many of his readers will not think that it makes up for the state-sponsored killing of millions of tiny human beings in their mothers' wombs.

Finally, and still on the subject of big game hunting, though I may be lacking in moral sensibility, I cannot see it as a great advance that we should speak today of 'antelopes' where our grandfathers or great-grandfathers might have spoken of 'antelope' (ibid.).

More confusion

If his particular examples of the moral progress made by a society increasingly 'emancipated' from Christianity do not greatly inspire us, what of his astonishing claim (p. 271) that the very notion of a common humanity, shared by human beings of both sexes and all races, is 'deeply unbiblical', and a product of modern biology? This is the very reverse of the truth. The book of Genesis, which the Catholic Church maintains to be historically true, teaches the common ancestry of all human beings from a single human couple. What firmer basis for a common humanity, and so for universal moral principles, could one desire? It is the atheistic evolutionists who have tried to

---

[33] I shan't discuss the author's assumption that universal suffrage is a good in itself, but it is worth noting that it is an assumption. It is not self-evident that all adults in any given society, regardless of their responsibilities, level of education or philosophy of life, should have an equal say in choosing the society's rulers.

stamp out belief in our father Adam and our mother Eve. What's more, Professor Dawkins admits elsewhere that his evolutionary theory has no place for a fixed human nature. He explicitly declares (p. 301), 'there are no natural borderlines in evolution'. In other words, 'because of our evolutionary continuity with chimpanzees' (p. 300), there is a sliding scale of 'humanness', such that a being may be more human or less, depending upon its place on the scale. It is easy to see how such theories could lead to the worst kind of racial discrimination, however much our author would deplore this.

Anti-Christian writers of modern times have, in fact, been guilty of the most extravagant racism. Professor Dawkins quotes a truly shocking passage from H. G. Wells, in which Wells apparently recommends the extermination of non–white races (pp. 269-70). Yet strangely enough, our author doesn't seem to realize how much this quotation tells against his contention that secular morals are superior to Christian ones. He naively comments, 'And Wells was regarded as a progressive in his own time' – as if Wells' Christian contemporaries would have suggested even more appalling schemes of extermination than he did! Is it necessary to point out that no one with a vestige of Christian sentiment, let alone belief, could ever have shared Wells' desire to 'kill the inferior races'?

In exactly the same confused manner, Professor Dawkins mentions that 'Washington, Jefferson and other men of the enlightenment held slaves' (p. 267). Insofar as one can reconstruct his thought, he seems to mean something like this: 'These men of the enlightenment must have had better morals than the Christian civilization that preceded them, since otherwise it wouldn't be called "the enlightenment"; but we're better than they were, as well as less Christian, since we don't keep slaves; therefore the further we go from Christian civilization, the better we become.' In fact, of course, it was precisely the slave-owning habits of the American colonists that so shocked such a great representative of Christian civilization as Samuel Johnson. Here again, by a happy incompetence, our author has chosen an example of moral change that tells in our favour and not in his. What his examples really show is that the secular conscience is liable to aberrations from which the Christian conscience is protected. The slave-owning of Jefferson, the ravings of H. G. Wells, are condemned now by the secular conscience itself; but in their day it was Christians who opposed them. Today, the spiritual heirs of Jefferson and Wells propose homosexual marriage and rights for chimpanzees: the secularists of two hundred years hence, if any are then in existence, are likely to think these things as incredible as Catholics think them now.

Chapter 8

PROFESSOR DAWKINS AND THE CATHOLIC CHURCH

Professor Dawkins' attack on religion is principally, though not exclusively, an attack on Christianity. He himself acknowledges that this is so (p. 37). So he impugns, as we have seen, the morals and historical accuracy of the Bible, but not the Koran or the Vedic scriptures. In addition, he is at some pains to ridicule the developed doctrines of Christianity, and perhaps in particular the doctrines of Catholicism. He tells us quite frankly (p. 316), 'For all sorts of reasons I dislike the Roman Catholic Church': an avowal that is not, I think, made quite so bluntly about any other, named religion. Nevertheless, since he adds, 'but I dislike unfairness even more', perhaps he will be ready to re-examine his criticisms of Catholic doctrines and acknowledge the various errors into which his book has fallen.

Theological language

Our author dislikes the vocabulary of Catholic theology. This is his prerogative; but I am sorry to say that his objection is nothing more profound than the old complaint about theology being a matter of 'splitting hairs' (p. 33). It seems odd for a biologist to use this particular metaphor pejoratively: surely it is the glory of biology to analyze nature more finely than the naked eye, splitting hairs and even genes? In any case, all this charge amounts to is that theology speaks about God precisely. How would he prefer it to speak about Him? Of course, he is unwilling to admit that God exists in the first place; but surely he would at least acknowledge that if there were a transcendent and perfect Creator of the universe, it would be desirable to speak about Him in an accurate rather than a vague manner. He complains that the language of theology is often impenetrable to the outsider; but would a man without training in biology walk into a lecture given by Professor Dawkins at the Examination Schools and hope to understand straightaway whatever he heard? Not if he was wise. Just as biology has its own proper vocabulary for describing its subject matter, so also does theology, and so does every other discipline. He may not admit that theology has a subject matter; that it is another question, and one that we have already examined. But it is entirely unreasonable to complain that it uses technical terms.

In reality, our author greatly exaggerates the difficulty of theological language. He quotes the following exposition of the doctrine of the Trinity from St Gregory Thaumaturgus, a third century Greek bishop and theologian:

> There is therefore nothing created, nothing subject to another in the Trinity: nor is there anything that has been added as though it once had not existed, but had entered afterwards: therefore the Father has never been without the Son, nor the Son without the Spirit: and this same Trinity is immutable and unalterable for ever.

He comments sarcastically, 'whatever miracles may have

earned St Gregory his nickname,[34] they were not miracles of honest lucidity. His words convey the character-istically obscurantist flavour of theology' (p. 34). Now, I suppose I spend more time with theological authors than Professor Dawkins does; but even taking into account my greater familiarity with such language, I cannot see what he objects to in these words. The saint's exposition is perfectly lucid. He tells us that the Trinity is God, not something created, and hence that no divine person can act upon another. He tells us that God the Trinity has always been the same and always will be the same without changing in any way. What is 'obscurantist' about that? This passage from St Gregory is mysterious, of course, since God is beyond our comprehension; but it is not particularly difficult. Still less does its author seek to conceal his meaning or blur the outlines of his ideas, as the charge of obscurantism implies.

The truth is, our author does not want to understand what the theologians are saying. On p. 33 he quotes the definition of the Council of Nicaea that the Son is 'consubstantial with the Father', and writes 'What on earth could that possibly mean? . . . "Very little" seems the only reasonable reply.' If he had consulted a work of Catholic theology, he would have found that it means simply that the Son is God in the same sense as the Father, not in an inferior sense. He throws up his hands when theologians use words like 'essence' and 'substance', as if they were empty terms, invented to impress the ignorant faithful. Yet on p. 193 he is happily talking about the essence of memes!

---

[34] The surname *Thaumaturgus* comes from the Greek for 'worker of wonders'.

Sometimes he seems scarcely to listen to himself, let alone to the theologians. So he writes that 'rivers of mediaeval ink' were squandered in suppressing the heretical notions of Arius about the Trinity, and at the end of the same paragraph he explains that Arius was a fourth century inhabitant of Alexandria, whose writings 'split Christendom down the middle for a century' (p. 33). Did the fourth century occur in the Middle Ages? This is not an author who has taken great pains to master his subject.

No Popery

If his attack on theological language puts our author in the school of rationalists like Voltaire or Edward Gibbon, at other times he seems more like a pupil of John Calvin. He makes the easy, but patently untrue, jibe that the veneration of the saints in the Catholic Church is polytheism in all but name (p. 34). A reasonable person might have supposed that the members of a given religion knew what they believed. After all, Professor Dawkins does not tell Orthodox Jews that they do not really suppose the Torah came from heaven, or Muslims that they do not really look forward to a resurrection. Why then does he tell Catholics that they are not really monotheists? The first article of the Nicene Creed makes it plain that we are. The fact that we ask the saints to pray for us no more detracts from our belief in one God than the fact that we ask good people on earth to pray for us. Yet he writes, apparently in all seriousness, that the Catholic Church 'pushes its recurrent flirtation with polytheism towards runaway inflation'. Is it not strange to see in what quarters the dead polemic of the Reformation lingers on?

Professor Dawkins absurdly attributes 'polytheistic hankerings' to Pope John Paul II (p. 35), on the ground that this pontiff attributed his survival of the assassination attempt of May 1981 to the Blessed Virgin Mary. Naturally, the Pope, like any Catholic, presupposes the universal causality of the one God whenever he speaks of a saint's 'doing' this or that. In precisely the same way, we presuppose God's universal causality whenever we speak of the actions of someone on earth. When we say, 'John has opened the front door', we have not suddenly become polytheists, suggesting that John could be a source of activity independent of God. Likewise, if a Catholic says, 'this or that saint saved my life', he simply means that God willed that the prayers of this particular saint, prayers that He Himself inspires, would be a reason for which his life would be saved. As for the heavy weather that our author makes of the Pope's reference to 'Our Lady of Fatima' in this context, John Paul's meaning, if he wishes to know, was that the shooting took place on that particular feast day (May 13th), and that part of the reason, in the Pope's opinion, why his life was spared was that the message of Fatima might be more widely disseminated.

Incidentally, on a related subject, what can our author mean by speaking of the 'four choirs of Angelic Hosts arrayed in nine orders' (p. 35)? The orders are familiar, though their precise number and distinction are hardly matters of faith; and I am afraid that we must decline the back-handed compliment of having 'nonchalantly' invented them, since St Gregory and Dionysius found them already in the Bible; but why does he say that they are divided into four choirs? The ancient writers generally spoke of three. Surely Professor Dawkins cannot have been granted a special revelation?

Some three hundred pages after attacking the Catholic Church for honouring the saints and angels, the author turns, at last, to the great question of Indulgences. Here again, one has the momentary illusion of reading some Reformation tract, rather than the work of an up-to-date atheist. It should not be necessary after five hundred years of explanations, but clearly it still is, to say that the Church has never taught that indulgences could be bought for money (p. 358), nor claimed to specify the length of Purgatorial 'time' for which remission could be gained (ibid.). The Catholic doctrine on indulgences is briefly this. Sins, even when forgiven, may leave behind a 'debt' that needs to be paid to the divine justice. One who is in a state of grace may expiate this 'debt' on earth by penitential works such as fasting and alms-giving; or else he may have to expiate it in purgatory. An indulgence is neither a pardon for sins committed nor (of course) a permission to commit sins, but rather an extra help towards expiating this debt of justice to God. It may be granted to a Catholic on his performing some officially designated 'good work'. The designated good work will always be some act done for the honour of God, such as reciting certain prayers or going on pilgrimage.

At certain periods in the past, designated 'good works' included the endowment of particular schools, hospitals or churches. Thus, certain Popes attached 'indulgences', which are only of value to those who confess and sincerely repent of their sins, to such benefactions. This was not 'paying for indulgences', any more than bringing a bottle of wine to the house of a friend is paying for his hospitality. Even so, in order to give no handle to the enemies of the Church, Pope Pius V decided in the sixteenth century that indulgences would no longer be attached to acts of almsgiving, despite the inevitable loss of revenues that this would cause charitable institutions.

Nor did the grants of so many days or weeks specified by particular indulgences refer to days or weeks in Purgatory itself. They were simply a convenient way of assigning the *relative* value of different indulgences. Thus to designate an indulgence as, say, 'a remission of twenty days', simply meant that it had twice the value of an indulgence of 'ten days'. It did not imply that the recipient was being guaranteed this number of days' remission of purgatory. How, one might ask, did the terminology of days and years arise in the first place? It was a throwback to the earliest centuries of the Church, when bishops sometimes remitted the public penance required of a penitent by a specified length of time in view of the merits of a local martyr. In other words, the doctrine of indulgences is based on the Catholic belief in the 'Communion of Saints': the fact that the merits of one member of the faithful can benefit other members, even if they are not known to each other personally.

Still on the subject of Purgatory, our author professes himself astonished by the evidence that Catholic theologians have offered for the existence of this intermediate state. Armed with the 1911 Catholic Encyclopaedia, he complains that the section entitled 'proofs' in the entry for 'Purgatory' simply mentions the Church's custom of praying for the dead. He takes this as a sign of our intellectual bankruptcy, naively concluding, 'this seriously is an example of what passes for reasoning in the theological mind' (p. 360). We might well retort:

'and this is an example of what passes for research with the prejudiced mind'. When it describes the Church's practice of praying for the dead as a 'proof' of Purgatory, the Encyclopaedia is not, of course, addressing itself to those who do not even admit the existence of a God! It is speaking to Christians who admit the tradition of the Church, in particular the tradition of the first centuries, as authoritative, and giving them proof that the faithful have believed in Purgatory, even without using the name, from the earliest times.

Original sin and atonement

In another section of his book, Professor Dawkins attacks the doctrine of original sin as 'vindictive' (p. 251) and that of vicarious atonement for sin as 'vicious' (pp. 252-3). I am somewhat reluctant to comment on these particular pages, since here more than elsewhere our author has made a special effort to give offence. Nevertheless, for the sake of completeness I shall respond. It is also possible that the author has never heard the Catholic statement of these two doctrines. He tells us (p. 11) that his own upbringing was in the Church of England; and the denominations, such as the Anglican Communion, that derive in some way from the Protestant Reformation have often put forward versions of these two doctrines that differ significantly from the Catholic teaching. Naturally, that would not excuse the language that he inflicts on his readers in these pages.

Original sin, then, is not understood by Catholics as a kind of personal guilt for which each succeeding generation would need to repent. Nor is it an arbitrary punishment of one person for another person's sin. It is the state in which human nature finds itself when left to itself. According to the Catholic faith, we are born lacking certain special privileges that our first parents did possess. These privileges included such things as the easy mastery of the emotions by the reason, and immunity to sickness. Such things were not due to human nature; they were gifts added to it. Because of the primordial sin, which took from our first parents both these gifts themselves and the power of passing them to their descendants, we are born without these privileges. Nevertheless, we have all that is due to our human nature. Nor do we have to repent of lacking these things, since it is no fault of ours that we don't have them. Why, it might be asked, did God make the fortunes of the race dependent on a single man? Catholics will reply that He willed to honour our first father by giving him the power to pass on his own privileges to his descendants, provided he persevered in friendship with God. He willed that Adam should be the spiritual, as well as the physical, father of the human race. But the necessary consequence of this divine choice was that if Adam did not persevere in God's friendship, then his descendants would not receive these extra blessings of body and soul.

As for vicarious atonement, Catholics do not understand this to mean that God punished His Son for the sins of men. By definition, only a guilty man may be justly punished. The Catholic doctrine of atonement depends not on the notion of punishment but on that of satisfaction. Sin shatters the relation between the creature and the Creator. Of course it cannot harm God in Himself, since He is immutable. But it violates His eternal right, as the supreme good, to be loved above all things. It thereby 'robs' God of the honour that is His due. To satisfy for sins is to restore the balance that should exist between creature and Creator, by taking something from oneself and offering it to Him, out of love for His supreme goodness. The Catholic teaching, based not only upon St Paul as our author claims but also upon the gospels,[35] is that Jesus Christ made a perfect satisfaction for sins by the offering of His life. He was not 'punished' by God, since He was without sin. He offered His life to God, and this gift, being the life of a divine person and therefore of infinite value, glorified God more than all human sins had insulted Him.

Professor Dawkins asks, 'If God wanted to forgive our sins, why not just forgive them?' (p. 253). If he really desires an answer to that question, he might consult, for example, St Thomas Aquinas' *Summa Theologiæ*.[36] There he will find it explained that whilst God could have dealt with the Fall by ways other than the incarnation and passion of Christ, no other way would have given us so great an example of charity or so great an incentive to avoid future sins, nor would any other have so promoted the dignity of human nature, a man restoring what a man had lost.

Faith and reason

Our author seems entirely innocent of the Catholic teaching on the relation between faith and reason. Intending to describe a typical 'religious' attitude, he offers the following statements:

> Faith (belief without evidence) is a virtue. The more your beliefs defy the evidence, the more virtuous you are. Believers who believe something unsupported and insupportable in the

---

[35] See, for example, Mk 10:45 and Jn 10:15-18.
[36] Third Part, question 46, article 3.

teeth of evidence and reason are especially highly rewarded. (p. 199)[37]

Note that he is not simply claiming that religious beliefs are in fact irrational. He is claiming that *believers themselves* hold that their beliefs lack any evidence and may well be contrary to reason. Later on, he specifically asserts that Christianity teaches that there is no need to justify belief on any rational ground (p. 306). Whilst this may be true of some groups that make 'personal experience' the ground for faith, it is not, of course, the view of the Catholic Church. We consider that it is possible to make a rational case for the truth of the Catholic faith, and that it is impossible that any truth of faith should be contrary to a truth of reason.

Professor Dawkins supposes that because we say that faith is a virtue, therefore we must consider our religion incapable of rational justification. So he will write, 'What is really pernicious is the practice of teaching children that faith itself is a virtue. Faith is an evil precisely because it requires no justification' (pp. 307-8). But the question of whether faith is a virtue is entirely separate from the question of whether the doctrine accepted by faith requires or permits of rational justification. To make the Catholic position clear, we need to consider two cases: first of someone who was not baptized and not brought up as a Catholic from infancy, and secondly of someone who was.

We hold that at least by the time that he reaches adulthood, the person who has not been brought up as a

---

[37] I have omitted from this quotation a few words intended to express an insult rather than a thought.

Catholic should know, by reason and not by faith, certain truths about God: in particular, that He exists and that He is to be obeyed. But such a person could not normally be expected to embrace the Catholic faith simply because someone told him to. Normally, some public fact will be necessary to give him a rational motive for belief. This public fact could be a miracle that he witnesses in person, performed by a teacher of the faith. More commonly, it would be the facts of Christ's life and the history of the Church – not, however, as accepted on faith, but as objects of rational, historical knowledge.

If this person comes to the stage of judging by the light of reason, 'the Church is from God, and so her teaching is worthy of belief', he can then receive from God the virtue of faith by which he will actually believe the things that the Church puts forward for our acceptance. This virtue, which he will then receive unless he is ill-disposed in his heart towards God, is a supernatural light that assures him of the truth of the Church's teaching. From the moment that he possesses this light, it becomes wrong for him to begin again to question the truth of the Church's teaching, since that would be tantamount to doubting the veracity of God. The rational justification of the Catholic faith was a ladder by which he climbed to the point where he could receive the internal gift of faith. Having once received this gift, he has no more need of the ladder for himself, though he can still make it available for others. So St Peter tells his converts, 'Be always ready to satisfy everyone that asks you a reason of the hope that is in you' (1 Pet 3:15).

Children who have been baptized in infancy, however, are not in the same position as adults who are still finding their way to the Church. The Church holds that they receive the light of faith by the very fact of baptism. Thus, when they're brought up, their teachers don't need to prove to them why they ought to become Catholics, as they are Catholics already. The task of their teachers is to present to them those truths which, by the fact of their baptism, they already have sufficient light for accepting. Since they already have the light of faith, it would be wrong for them to entertain doubts about whether the faith is true. Still, as the children grow older, they should be taught rational apologetics, not principally for their own sake, but so that they may be able to help non-Catholics enquirers. Professor Dawkins would no doubt reply that he doesn't believe that God does anything to a child's soul in baptism; disbelieving in God and the soul, he could hardly say anything else. Still, if he considers the Catholic position closely he will find that the statements 'Catholics should not allow themselves to doubt their faith' and 'Baptized children should be taught the faith as something certain' do not contradict the statement 'Catholicism is capable of rational justification'.

Cruelty to children

Our author entitles one of his chapters 'Childhood, Abuse and Religion'.[38] It ranges widely, and contains a number of statements with which no Catholic need disagree, as that the Incas ought not to have worshipped the sun (p. 328), and that P. G. Wodehouse was an outstanding writer of humorous prose (pp. 343-4). He does, however, offer two pieces of evidence intended to prove that Catholic doctrines lead to cruelty to children, and these

---

[38] pp. 311-44.

seem to require some comment.[39]

The first is the 'Mortara case'. Edgardo Mortara was born to Jewish parents in Bologna in 1851. When still a baby, he became seriously ill. Fearing that he would die, the Mortaras' Catholic maid secretly baptized him, in accordance with canon law. The boy then made a surprising recovery. When Edgardo was six, the Archbishop of Bologna learned of the matter, and on the instructions of Pope Pius IX, who was then the civil ruler of that part of Italy, the boy was removed from his family home to be educated as a Catholic lest he be taught to renounce his baptism and reject Christ.

Naturally, our author fulminates against this action by the last pope but nine. It was an act of 'shattering cruelty' (p. 315), or again, of 'grotesque cruelty', attributable – of course – to the 'crass insensitivity' of 'celibate priests' (ibid.). We can certainly agree that the case was a tragic one. But why does he not include any testimony from the principal party concerned? He writes that 'what mattered to Edgardo was not "his" religion . . . but the love and care of his parents and family', implying that the boy was kept from them against his will. In fact, a very brief amount of research on the internet – and the author's book includes

---

[39] Our author's thought processes, here as elsewhere, are hard to follow. He writes that he deliberately refrains from 'detailing the horrors of the Crusades . . . or the Spanish Inquisition' in order to describe evils that arise from the religious mind 'specifically because it is religious' (pp. 312-3). But why does he suppose that the Crusades and the Spanish Inquisition did not proceed from religious minds specifically as religious? It is difficult to avoid the suspicion that he simply could not be bothered to do any research into these two topics, mentioning them only to fling some mud at the Church in passing.

numerous citations from this source – reveals that this was not so, as we shall now see.

Edgardo Mortara went on to become a priest and a religious, and he took the name 'Pio' out of gratitude towards the Pope who educated him. Much later, when the cause for the beatification of Pius IX was being conducted, Fr Mortara was called as the twenty-seventh witness. Speaking under oath, he gave the following description of what happened one week after he had been brought at the Pope's instructions from his family house in Bologna to Rome:

> My parents presented themselves to the Institute of Neophytes to initiate the complex procedures to get me back in the family. As they had complete freedom to see me and talk with me, they remained in Rome for a month, coming every day to visit me. Needless to say, they tried every means to get me back – caresses, tears, pleas and promises. Despite all this, I never showed the slightest desire to return to my family, a fact which I do not understand myself, except by looking at the power of supernatural grace. [40]

Does Professor Dawkins think that the young Edgardo should have been forced against his will to be brought up a Jew, rather than a Catholic, as he himself desired? If so, what has become of his own 'third Commandment', that children must be allowed to disagree with their parents? Whatever one thinks of this exceptional case, the reality was far distant from the lurid picture that our author paints of heartless inquisitors inflicting psychological torment

---

[40] http://www.zenit.org/english/archive/documents/Mortara-PioIX. html. The report from which this paragraph is extracted has been available on the internet since September 20th 2000, or six years before Professor Dawkins' book was published.

upon a helpless child.

The other piece of evidence that he brings against the Catholic Church to support his charge of 'doctrinal cruelty' is that it teaches children to believe in hell. He writes that he is 'persuaded that the phrase "child abuse" is no exaggeration when used to describe' this practice (p. 318).[41] To justify this persuasion, he calls upon three witnesses, two of whom had been raised as Catholics (pp. 317–8, 321), the third as a member of a group called 'the Exclusive Brethren' (pp. 321–2). All are quoted as saying that they were terrified by the teaching that they received on this subject as children; two say that they still suffer from its ill effects as adults.

Now, by this method of arguing, one could 'prove' that almost any form of education constituted abuse. For example, let us suppose that I found three former students of biology from three different universities who had all suffered mental anguish during their preparations for their final examinations, two of whom still had nightmares about sitting these exams unprepared. Would Professor Dawkins be willing to accept this as proof that teaching biology to university students is abuse of vulnerable adults? If not, by what right does he assert that Catholics who teach the catechism are abusing children?

Again, it would be very easy, by our author's method, to prove that marriage is a form of abuse. One would

---

[41] He does not explicitly mention the Catholic Church in this paragraph: nevertheless, he would seem to have it in mind, since he specifies that the doctrine to which he objects is that 'unshriven mortal sins' lead to final loss. The term 'unshriven' refers to the Catholic doctrine of confession to a priest, which is not shared, for example, by Protestant bodies or by Islam.

simply have to find three people who said that their spouses had treated them very badly, two of whom said that the memory of it was extremely painful. If one is determined to ignore all examples of happily married people or all children who were instructed in the four last things without lasting damage, then naturally one will bring against the Church a verdict of 'guilty'.

The truth, of course, is that teaching children, like any other activity, can be done well or badly. A number of subjects require particularly delicate handling when broached with a child or adolescent, for example the questions of sex or death. If these subjects are not well taught, it is easy to imagine that a child may suffer as a result, or even be marked for life by information imparted in a wrong way or at a wrong age. But I don't suppose that the author would argue that no one should be given any teaching on these two subjects. In the same way, the Catholic doctrine of the possibility of final separation from God needs to be taught with particular care when the hearers are children. The teacher needs to ensure, for example, that the children don't suppose that their minor misdemeanours are mortal sins. Still, it is quite possible to teach the doctrine in such a way that the normal child – for those who are unusually or morbidly sensitive cannot set the rule for the whole group – is not terrified or 'traumatized' by what he hears. Most children will be chastened by this teaching, but that is not the same thing as being terrified, as any parent knows. And whilst I can't speak for a group such as the Exclusive Brethren, this subject occupies only a small part of the religious instruction traditionally assigned for Catholic school-children. For example, the 'Catechism of Christian Doctrine', a booklet designed for older children and approved for use by the English bishops since 1889, contains 370 short questions and answers. Of these 370, only six relate, in the briefest possible terms, to the possibility of final loss.[42] No description of this state is given. Nor does the catechism encourage children to make hell their motive for avoiding sins, but rather the goodness and mercy of God.

Finally, one can remark that while children need suffer no harm by learning about the awesome power of their free will, both children and adults will suffer grave moral damage if taught to believe that their notions of good and evil have no objective basis, and are simply those that enabled their ancestors' genes to reproduce.

---

[42] The questions are numbers 122, 125, 134, 344, 349 and 351. One might add number 292, though this is a reassurance against an exaggerated idea of the dispositions necessary for sacramental absolution.

Chapter 9

THE TWO WAYS

We have now finished our survey of Professor Dawkins' book. It seems fitting by way of conclusion to sum up the two 'philosophies of life' contrasted throughout these pages: secular atheism and Catholicism (I speak of 'secular atheism' rather than simply of atheism to distinguish our author's philosophy from those systems, such as Buddhism, that deny God but teach some form of human survival after death.)

The secular atheists, of which group Professor Dawkins is today among the chief English-speaking representatives, make matter the first of all things. Matter, brute stuff, is for them the source whence flows life, intelligence, the arts, love, justice and all the desires that may fill the human heart. The Catholic considers it absurd to claim that matter, which is assuredly the least of things, can give rise to all these things so much greater than itself. He considers it absurd to say that something can give what it does not possess, and that the greater can be caused by the less. We hold, accordingly, that mind is the first of things, being at once simpler and more perfect than matter.

The atheist of Professor Dawkins' school holds that man came into being undesigned. He imagines that the human race derives from the twin principles of Chance and Necessity, chance variations in matter being necessarily either preserved or lost as they aided or hindered reproduction. The Catholic holds it absurd to claim that the mind of man resulted from any such blind process. If our mental powers had been established on the sole principle of reproductive utility, there would be no guarantee that they could grasp the truth and all thinking would be in vain. Unless our minds were designed in order to reason truly, we could have no confidence in their veracity, since they would ultimately be under the sway of some non-rational force. But only what is rational itself can design a rational being. Therefore, since everyone's own consciousness assures him that his mind does indeed grasp truth, the human mind must depend upon some transcendent Intellect. This Intellect, being the first of things, is unlimited, since there is nothing prior to It that might impose any boundary upon It.

The atheist can find no place in his philosophy for duty, that is, for a law obliging men to obey it, even if it should contradict all human laws. For such a law implies the existence of a law-giver superior to mankind. Denying God, therefore, the atheist denies objective morality. He may say that he prefers to educate his children rather than to torture them, but he cannot say that he has a duty to do the one and to avoid the other.

Lacking a notion of duty, the atheist cannot rationally blame those who act in ways contrary to himself. He can threaten murderers and child-abusers with prison, but not tell them that they have acted wrongly or have a duty to change their ways. He cannot speak with moral authority, for he recognizes none.

The Catholic, by contrast, believes with the best of the gentiles, in 'the unwritten, unalterable laws of God and heaven'.[43] He holds that we have not only a preference but also a duty to feed a child rather than to torture it, or to defend our country rather than betray it into the hands of an enemy. He holds that such laws exist before all human deliberation, and that our knowledge of them is implanted within us by the uncreated Intelligence who made our minds. This moral law can never be entirely blotted out from man's heart, even though vehement desires or others' bad examples may obscure it in part and for a time.

Likewise, the consistent atheist must reject the emotion of shame. If a bad act were simply the transgression of a useful principle, its perpetrator might reasonably feel regret for having made a mistake, or fear at the thought of reprisals from some wider group, but not shame: the sense of having done that which it is not right to do. Shame is a distinctive, irreducible thing, neither regret nor fear. It implies an acceptance of the unalterable laws binding us in conscience. If there be no eternal laws, but only human conventions and useful hereditary traits, shame is an aberration. Logically, the atheist must be shameless, that is, inhuman.

The atheist holds that religion, of all kinds and in all ages, is a delusion which can only not be called madness because it is so widespread. If he is of the school of Professor Dawkins, he must believe that the mainspring of lives so various and fruitful as St Paul's, St Benedict's, Dante's, Pascal's, Pasteur's, Dostoyevsky's, Cardinal Newman's or Mother Teresa's was the malfunctioning of some principle useful for the survival of our genes. The Catholic considers it absurd to hold that holiness and wisdom may arise by mistake; as if all the masterpieces in the art-galleries should arise from the slipping of their painters' hands.

---

[43] Sophocles' *Antigone*.

Nor need a Catholic be disconcerted by the great variety of religions in the world. We hold that God made man to know and love Him, but that this pure impulse, implanted in the human race at its creation, is resisted by many strong forces within and around us, which may wholly check it or turn it from its proper end.

The atheist holds that human life has no purpose, or, which amounts to the same thing, that it has only those purposes which individual human beings choose to give it. He cannot explain why, of all the creatures on the earth, only men look for some fulfilment beyond this life. He cannot explain why man, if he is only a product of the earth, is not content with what the earth has to offer. The Catholic holds that we were made for a definite goal, and that we remain at best imperfectly satisfied in this life because our goal lies beyond the grave. We were made to see God as He is, and since Adam's fall, no one may do this unless first he pass through death.

The secular atheist holds that death utterly extinguishes human personality. Since the continued existence of a rational being is a good, in fact an excellent thing, this philosophy leads to bravado or despair. Bravado, with those who claim to await annihilation with indifference; despair with those who do not suppress their natural desire for beatitude. The Catholic considers both these attitudes unworthy of man. Immortality is our proper destiny, for our minds are not material things. To think is not the action of a material thing, for no movement or attribute of matter could ever be accounted a thought. Since our minds are not material, they cannot be destroyed. To destroy a thing is to divide it into its components, and where there is no matter there can be no such division.

The human mind or soul is spiritual, therefore, and cannot share in the body's dissolution. It remains in perpetuity, with its power to know and to love, or also to hate. And though this cannot be verified by reason, the Catholic holds that the body will rise again, vivified by the same power that once created the world, to share in the immortality of the soul.

The atheist is logically obliged to reject free will. This is especially clear if he is, like most Western atheists, a materialist. Since every event has a cause, our bodily actions also must have a cause. But if all is matter, then our bodily actions are caused by matter. Now matter does not act for any purpose of its own, but by necessity: water does not flow downhill because it has chosen to, but because it must. Therefore, if all is matter, our bodily actions happen by necessity, and free will is an illusion. But if free will is an illusion, we need pay no attention to those who argue for atheism, since they cannot be thinking and writing as men guided by the truth, but only as driven along by matter.

The Catholic, supported by the spontaneous consent of all mankind, holds that man is free. His actions therefore derive from some power within him that is not material but immaterial or spiritual, namely, his will. But if there were no God, I could not possess any such spiritual power. For my will did not exist before I did; nor, since it is not material, is it composed of pre-existing parts. It follows that a will, as also an intellect, must be freshly created for each new man who comes into being. Only God can do such a thing. If then we believe in freedom, we must also believe in God.

Yet though man is free, he is not a law unto himself. God who makes his will has the right to command him how to use it. We must follow the law of good and evil that He has impressed upon our heart, and be ready to welcome those whom He may send to teach us about His will. And since no wise lawgiver promulgates a law without intending that its provisions be enforced, we shall be judged by God on the use that we make of our free will.

These, then, are two philosophies, capable of building two cities. On the one hand, our author's: a philosophy that reduces all things to matter, and so can explain neither reason, nor freedom, nor the desires of the human heart, nor morals, nor duty, nor shame. It leaves man without God, without hope and without honour. Nor can it explain even matter itself. For if the whole universe were simply one dense ball of matter, it would still be necessary to posit a spiritual Creator. Nothing with parts, that is, no material thing, can exist unless something causes its parts to exist together. That is why the first cause must be spiritual and simple.

On the other hand is our own, that is, the Catholic philosophy: not that it is held only by those incorporated into the Catholic Church, but that this Church has defined it more clearly than any other body. This philosophy recognizes that Mind is the first of things. The First Mind is unlimited and without parts, an eternal and subsistent Thought. Man, though only a creature of God, is made in His image, possessing both intelligence and freedom. He is not a product of chance, but of will, that is of Love. Since he has spiritual powers which cannot decay, he is made for immortality. Since spiritual powers are not restricted in their scope, he is capable of an infinite good, that is, of God Himself. Our proper destiny therefore is the immortal possession of the boundless good. Of this goal and happiness no man is deprived, save by his free choice.